D1251789

# You Can Make Music!

# YOU CAN MAKE MUSIC!

## It's Never Too Late to Start

ATARAH BEN-TOVIM & DOUGLAS BOYD

LONDON
VICTOR GOLLANCZ LTD
1986

First published in Great Britain 1986
by Victor Gollancz Ltd,
14 Henrietta Street, London WC2E 8QJ

*To Jennie Wilson and Ruari McNeill,
whose far-sightedness made possible the
initial research on which this book is based.*

*British Library Cataloguing in Publication Data*
Ben-Tovim, Atarah
    You can make music: it's never too late to start
    1. Music — Performance
    I. Title     II. Boyd, Douglas
    780′.7′1          MT170
    ISBN 0 575 03782 2
    ISBN 0 575 03783 0 pbk

Photoset by Rowland Phototypesetting Limited
Bury St Edmunds, Suffolk
Printed in Great Britain by St Edmundsbury Press Limited
Bury St Edmunds, Suffolk

# CONTENTS

# *You Can Make Music!*

Nine out of ten music-lovers admit that one of their greatest regrets is being unable to play an instrument. YOU CAN MAKE MUSIC! is more than just the title of this book; it is a statement of fact.

If you find it difficult to believe, answer the following three questions:

Do you consider yourself a music-lover?                    YES/NO

Is listening to music an important pleasure in
your life?                                                YES/NO

Have you said or thought many times: "I wish I
could play a musical instrument"?                         YES/NO

If you answered YES to all three questions, but cannot make music because you never learned to play an instrument, there must be reasons why. Probably, your reasons are among those on the next page.

*"I cannot play a musical instrument because. . . ."*

|  | Tick reasons which apply |
|---|---|
| 1. It's too difficult for me. | |
| 2. I had piano/violin lessons as a child, but I gave up because I was no good at music. | |
| 3. I'm too old to start learning anything new. | |
| 4. It doesn't seem worth all the hard work of learning, when I could never be as good as Menuhin/Oscar Peterson/John Williams etc. | |
| 5. You have to learn to read music and I could never do that. | |
| 6. It is necessary to start learning in childhood. | |
| 7. I enjoy listening to music, but I'm not musical enough to *play* an instrument. | |
| 8. I've always fancied the oboe/cello etc., but I've heard it's too difficult. | |
| 9. (I was told at school that) I am tone deaf. | |
| 10. (I have seen so many prodigies and virtuosi on television that) I know I'm not talented enough. | |

Whether you ticked one, or all ten of the reasons why, does not matter.

How valid are these reasons which have stopped you from achieving your natural desire to make music?

Let's examine them, one by one.

"It's too difficult for me."

Learning to play an instrument to amateur level need be no more difficult than learning to drive a car, or touch-type or do *cordon bleu* cookery. A couple of generations ago, most well-educated adults made music for their own pleasure. Millions of children do it without realizing that it is

8

supposed to be difficult. On p. 22, there is a Skill and Motivation Test by which you can measure whether it really is too difficult for you.

"I had piano/violin lessons as a child, but I gave up because I was no good at music."

Most children who begin music lessons give up because they start at a wrong time or on an unsuitable instrument. This "failure" has nothing to do with being good or otherwise at music, although tragically most of them will continue to believe they are "no good at music" for life.

"I'm too old to start anything new."

This reason is used by sixteen-year-olds as frequently as by sixty-year-olds! In fact, older students usually amaze themselves and their teachers by their rapid progress. The age of the learner is not important; choosing the right time to begin, is. By using the Right Time Test on p. 16, you can check whether this is the right time for you.

"It doesn't seem worth all the hard work of learning, when I know I could never be as good as Menuhin/Oscar Peterson/John Williams etc."

It can take courage to put aside the sound of great professional players, yet every amateur player knows that the deep satisfaction and pleasure of playing within one's own potential far outweigh the joys of simply listening to the greatest players on record.

"You have to learn to read music and I couldn't do that."

Learning to read the music of some instruments, e.g. the piano, *is* very hard, but there are other instruments whose music is very easy to read. On them, the adult learner just 'picks up' notation as he learns instrumental technique. Unbelievable? It is to anyone who, as a child had to grapple for years unsuccessfully with piano notation, but it's true.

"It is necessary to start learning in childhood."

Except for the stringed instruments, the reverse is more likely to be true. In practice, what takes a six- or eight-year-old two or three years to master, is achieved by adult learners *within weeks*. Adults have one tremendous advantage over children learning instruments: all instruments were designed to fit the fully-grown adult body and only guitar, violin and cello can be made in child-sizes. All the physical problems which delay children's progress, and often lead to giving up altogether, can be ignored by adults.

"I enjoy listening to music, but I'm not musical enough to *play* an instrument."

Most non-players over-estimate the degree of musical ability neccessary to play an instrument. On p. 19 there is a Musicality Test which you can use to measure how musical you are. Most adults are musical enough to play some instruments; many adults are musical enough to play any instrument.

"I've always fancied the oboe/cello, etc, but I've heard that it's too difficult."

Some musical instruments are technically far more difficult than others. Part II of this book sets out clearly which are the difficult instruments and enables you to choose the instrument which best suits you.

"(I was told at school that) I am tone deaf."

Many thousands of adults believe they are tone deaf. Almost all are wrong. Tone deafness is rarer than colour-blindness. It is impossible for anyone who gets pleasure from listening to music to be tone deaf, whatever they may have been told.

"(I have seen so many prodigies and virtuosi on television that) I know I'm not talented enough."

What makes a professional musician, a virtuoso or a prodigy has almost nothing to do with the qualities that make an amateur player. The amount of sheer talent required to become an amateur musician is within anyone who loves music and genuinely seeks a way of expressing this feeling.

*All the "reasons why" are based on misinformation! Even if you ticked all ten of them, they mean nothing at all. The important thing is whether you answered YES to all three questions on the first page. If you did, YOU CAN MAKE MUSIC!*

# How to choose the instrument on which you will succeed

How does the music-lover who wishes to begin making music set about choosing an instrument? There are only two ways: a random choice and a methodical, step-by-step approach.

Many random choices *sound* logical, but they are based on guesswork, mystique and misinformation. Examples are:

"I've always fancied playing the flute, but I never had time before."

"The piano is the most satisfying instrument for an adult to play."

"My son/daughter is having fun in guitar lessons at school, so I think I'll have a go."

If the reasoning is tenuous, well, there's always the feeling that music is rather mysterious and that, somehow, the magic ingredient will just appear one day, like the Lost Chord. Unhappily, if there is a magic powder, fewer than one in a hundred people find it; that is the statistical likelihood of success resulting from random choice of instrument.

The methodical approach, on the other hand, should be an unbiased consideration of the detailed possibilities and pleasures of all the instruments, an objective assessment of their difficulty to learn and play and an unprejudiced examination of their suitability for the one individual concerned. Few people try to make such a methodical approach on their own, because the necessary research and experimentation would take several years.

What is required is a system which assembles for the music-lover all the relevant facts about all the instruments and enables him or her to make a reasoned choice. The Ben-Tovim/Boyd System does all that—and it's fun. The System was designed to be used by any adult, however much or little he or she knows about music. Indeed, the basic work on the System was done by a professional musician who was a prodigy playing concertos with world-famous orchestras while still in her teens *and* a musical drop-out who gave up the piano after several agonizing years of weekly lessons.

The work on which the System is based was a unique programme of ten years' research during which the writers founded and ran the world's most comprehensive Music Research Centre: a forty-four room complex of studios, instrument-matching and assessment booths, interview rooms, recording and editing suites, teaching studios, rehearsal and practice rooms, performance areas, plus social areas, offices and facilities covering most aspects of music as a leisure activity.

The Centre was independent of the schools system, music colleges, universities and the arts establishment. It was run as a Charitable Trust. That independence was vital. It alone ensured that the staff were under no pressure to prove the prejudices or beliefs of any person or organization. It left us free to investigate without bias what people of all ages seek from music in their lives.

Although the first priority was to examine the musical needs of modern children—so different from what the schools system chooses to believe—our reputation in that field led to increasing numbers of adults seeking help. They came from all walks of life and had a surprising range of ages. What they had in common was a deeply-felt desire to release their frustrated musical potential. One and all, they felt they had been somehow cheated out of their musical birthright, that they had "missed out" on music.

Hundreds of personal counselling sessions with these adults involved psychologists, musicians, teachers and other specialists with whose expert help this System was devised for use by adults of all ages who have ever said, or felt: "I wish I could play an instrument."

In this book the framework of the System is a range of twenty-four instruments which are the most suitable and enriching for an adult to learn. There is no intention ever to "fit" the person to the instrument, but conversely to expose all the instruments one by one for examination and comparison by the would-be player. All the necessary information is to be found in the Information Sheets. To fill in the carefully-designed Tests and Score Cards requires no previous musical knowledge.

There are no "right" or "wrong" answers to the questions, nor is there any favouring of this or that instrument or kind of music, as against another. However, the System only works accurately if the user is reasonably honest and objective. If you are not, the

System will produce the right instrument for the person you are pretending to be!

There are two distinct parts to the System. In the first, the user checks his or her suitability to learn an instrument.

*Part I: The Preliminary Tests*

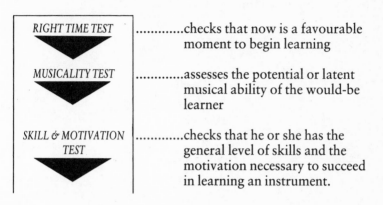

| | |
|---|---|
| RIGHT TIME TEST | .............checks that now is a favourable moment to begin learning |
| MUSICALITY TEST | .............assesses the potential or latent musical ability of the would-be learner |
| SKILL & MOTIVATION TEST | .............checks that he or she has the general level of skills and the motivation necessary to succeed in learning an instrument. |

If the results of the Preliminary Tests are satisfactory, then the user proceeds to . . .

*Part II: Selecting Your Instrument*

| | |
|---|---|
| INFORMATION SHEETS & SCORE CARDS FOR 24 INSTRUMENTS | .........give the essential facts about each instrument<br>.........are fun to fill in, yet doing so automatically produces a four-way assessment of each instrument |
| COMPARISON CHART | .........reveals at a glance which instruments are suitable or unsuitable to learn |
| THE ONE INSTRUMENT FOR YOU | .........is either "Top of the Chart", or one of three on the Short List. |

Having selected the right instrument, the adult beginner needs a wide range of information, which can be difficult to obtain. Answers are required to questions like:

"How much does an instrument cost?"

"How does one find a teacher?"

The Adult Beginner's Information Pack at the end of the book is a mini-directory of this kind of information.

# THE BEN-TOVIM / BOYD SYSTEM:

## PART I: THE PRELIMINARY TESTS

## *"Have you left it too late to start?"*

The first question most adults ask themselves is: "Have I left it too late to start learning an instrument?" They may feel that it is a long time since they studied a new subject, or that they no longer have the mental energy to begin something difficult. They may be suffering from misinformation in the media, which darkly hints that only a prodigy driven by powerful parents to practise eight hours a day throughout childhood can get anywhere in music.

There is no need to worry about having left it too late, for music is within almost everybody. It is not like an academic subject which has to be approached from outside. It is possible to begin making music with equal satisfaction and success at sixteen or sixty years of age—although the same person may well choose a different instrument at a different age.

The real question is not how old you are, but whether this is a favourable moment in your life to begin an important new activity. In every lifetime there are periods, not always obvious, when circumstances work against you, and others when they work in your favour. The prospect of making your own music is too important to risk mis-timing the start.

To check that now is a good time *for you*, use the Right Time Test below. All you have to do, is circle round the answers that apply to you. Don't be tempted to do the test mentally. As you work through the System, you will come to understand why it is important to make a mark on the paper as you answer each question.

| | | |
|---|---|---|
| 1. Do you feel the need for a new and progressive activity in your life? | NO | YES |
| 2. Do you find most canned entertainment on radio and television boring or unsatisfying? | NO | YES |
| 3. Would you like to have a new way of making social contacts with interesting people? | NO | YES |
| 4. Have you recently started a new job or more demanding work, or begun a new course of study, been promoted or moved house? | YES | NO |
| 5. Do you feel that "time is going very fast" and that you are not achieving very much at the moment? | NO | YES |
| 6. Have you recently entered a new relationship/got married/had a child/taken responsibility for an elderly relative? | YES | NO |
| 7. Have you given up or significantly reduced those physical activities (e.g. sports, walking) which you enjoyed when younger? | NO | YES |
| 8. Do you feel stale, or that you are stagnating, or that you have not learnt anything new for a long time? | NO | YES |
| 9. Have you spare energy and "time on your hands" which you did not have before, because of e.g. retirement, unemployment, children going to school, children leaving home, etc? | NO | YES |
| 10. Do you feel that your present way of life leaves an important part of your personality frustrated? | NO | YES |

Score:

To score in this Test, all you do is multiply by ten the number of times you circled a YES or NO *in the right-hand column.* Six circles in this column give a score of sixty, and so on.

If you scored 70 or over, now is the Right Time for you to begin making music. If you scored 50 or 60, it would probably be better to wait until some important element in your life changes, unless you score very highly in the Skill & Motivation Test.

If you scored below 50, carry on listening—or do Part II of the System for fun, as you might explore your own IQ. The one certain thing is that now is not the Right Time for you to begin an important new activity. If you do begin now, you are being unfair to yourself, and risk failing simply because you mis-timed your start.

## "How musical do you have to be?"

Many adults genuinely wonder whether they are musical enough to learn an instrument. Everything they read or hear about musicians in the Press, on radio and television, seems to hint at a great mystique—some elusive quality that makes a musician. "Do I have *it*?" they doubtingly wonder. "I love music, but am I musical enough to *make* it?"

Our personal counselling sessions revealed beyond a shadow of doubt that almost one hundred per cent of the general population is musical enough to learn to play a suitable instrument for their own pleasure. If listening to music is one of your most important leisure interests, it is virtually certain that you are one of the ninety-nine—not the odd man out.

Why do so many people ask the question? Why do they imagine the answer is going to be negative?

The most common reason is that many adults have suffered what can only be described as traumatic "musical accidents" in childhood or early life, which have reduced their musical self-confidence drastically. Some were forced to take lessons on unsuitable instruments, or instruments they disliked. Some were humiliated by being made to sing in public at the wrong time. Some detested school music lessons. (Most children still do.) Some were pressurised by a parent or teacher for years until they eventually gave up learning and accepted that they were "no good at music". In counselling, some of these adults told us sincerely that they were "tone deaf", that they could not sing or hum a recognizable tune, that they had no sense of rhythm, and so on. Yet, they were almost all able to learn a correctly chosen instrument once they had come to terms with the unfortunate previous experience.

Secondly, an adult who has listened for years to a great deal of recorded music may be subconsciously comparing his or her own imagined musical potential with the artistic achievement of Ashkenazi, James Galway or some other musical idol. It is one thing to recognize consciously the great difference between the qualities that make a virtuoso public performer and those necessary to play for one's own pleasure, but quite another to regain one's rightful musical self-confidence. How can an adult assess his or her own musicality?

Musicality, or musical potential, is a fascinating area. Surveys in seventeen countries during the past sixty years have produced consistent results. The countries were as various as Britain, the United States, East Africa, France, Sweden, Russia, Hungary, Germany. The findings of research organizations, universities, government departments and international cultural organizations may go some way to rebuilding any adult's damaged musical self-confidence. They indicate quite firmly that:

1. professional musicians are not more musical than dustmen or tax-collectors
2. advanced music students in music college and university are no more musical than their coevals reading maths or geography
3. any normal (i.e. not handicapped) person can learn to play an instrument, and many physically handicapped people make excellent progress on a carefully chosen instrument.

So, whatever musicality is, you almost certainly have enough of it, to make music on the right instrument. To verify this claim, no expensive apparatus, or pre-recorded cassettes of tones and chords are needed. Any pen or pencil will do to fill in the Musicality Test. This is not a test of your past musical achievements, musical knowledge, talent or aesthetic sensibility. It is a simple but reliable test which anyone can use to measure his or her own musicality. Don't worry if some of the questions seem too basic; we know what we're doing!

| | SCORE NIL | SCORE 10 EACH |
|---|---|---|
| 1. Can you quickly recognize the National Anthem, a favourite piece of music, or a popular television theme tune? | NO | YES |
| 2. If you hummed or whistled "God Save The Queen", could someone else recognize it? | NO | YES |
| 3. When listening, do you ever move to the music: tap a foot, drum your fingers, "conduct" to yourself, or dance? | NO | YES |
| 4. Can you name three professional musicians? | NO | YES |
| 5. Is listening to music an important pleasure in your life? | NO | YES |
| 6. Do you often sing, whistle, hum to yourself when alone, or sing along with radio, cassettes? | NO | YES |
| 7. Do you find it impossible to sing hee-haw with the hee very high and the haw very low? | YES | NO |
| 8. Do you find it difficult to march in step, or dance in time, to music? | YES | NO |
| 9. Each instrument has a characteristic sound. Some are easy to recognize; others more difficult. Can you identify the sound of eight or more of the following? FLUTE/PIANO/ELECTRIC GUITAR/TRUMPET/VIOLIN/ELECTRIC ORGAN/DRUM/HARP/SAXOPHONE/TROMBONE (Give yourself five marks if you could identify between five and seven of the instruments.) | NO | YES |
| 10. If you heard a short rhythm tapped on a drum or a table top, could you copy it back aloud?                        Score: | NO | YES |

To score, multiply by ten the number of times you circled a YES or NO in the right-hand column.

If you scored 70 or over, you are certainly musical enough to learn an instrument. It does not matter whether you have previously achieved anything musical in your life or not, for you have the potential to do it now. You should find a wide choice of instruments on which you could succeed.

A score of between 50 and 70 also means that you are musical enough to learn an instrument. Why the lower score? Think back to childhood or early life. Did you—like so many adults—suffer a musical accident of which you still bear the scars? If so, it is a great pity but not a reason to stop you beginning to make music now. However, you may need to take a little more care in your selection than someone with a higher score, in order to give yourself the best chance of success.

## "Is it too difficult for you?"

Every non-player wonders how difficult it is to learn a musical instrument.

Painful memories of childhood music lessons do not help anyone to assess just how easy or difficult it is. Nor does the mystique woven around the business of learning by most professional musicians and critics.

Here are the facts: any adult who wants to make music and who selects an instrument using this System will find that learning to play the instrument is a medium-difficult skill, roughly on a par with driving a car, touch-typing or cordon bleu cookery. It is easier than, for example, learning a language, doing major car repairs, making clothes or furniture without a kit or pattern.

Some instruments are more difficult than others to learn. The Information Sheets make it easy to avoid these, unless you are particularly attracted to one of them.

The problems which discourage most learners and eventually cause them to give up are nothing to do with the difficulties of the particular instrument; they are simply the result of random choice of instrument. Nine-tenths of the learners' energy goes into a hopeless battle against the essential incompatibility of themselves and the instruments they are trying to learn.

If you use the System to choose your instrument, you will not waste nine-tenths of your energy. Put another way, you will have ten times as much chance of succeeding.

That may sound like a claim for hair-restorer, but it works this way. When you play an instrument, it functions as an extension of your body. Nerves, muscles, tendons, diaphragm, lungs, the mouth, the hands—all work directly with parts of the instrument to produce a sound. Playing an instrument which "fits" your body and suits your mentality makes you feel good. The physical pleasure of playing the instrument and the mental and emotional rewards of making music are more than sufficient compensation for the work you are doing.

On the other hand, the physical stress of playing an instrument which does not "fit" you, or the lack of mental and emotional reward if the instrument cannot make the kind of music in the kind of situation you seek—eventually de-motivates all but the most stubborn learner, and results in failure.

As to how much time it takes, the answer varies, depending on the instrument; but most adults find that the System enables them to find an instrument, to learn which takes approximately the same amount of time and application as learning to drive a car. The average learner driver has twenty to thirty lessons, each lasting one hour—plus as much practice as possible—in order to pass the Driving Test. The same amount of lesson-time, with practice in between lessons, will get most adults off to an excellent start on an instrument selected using the System.

*Are you prepared to put as much effort into learning an instrument as you did into learning to drive?*

Most people experience a strong motivation to learn to drive. It is that motivation to succeed that carries them through the difficult periods when gear-changing or clutch-control, or whatever, seem impossible to master. Adults who doubt whether their motivation will last throughout the process of learning an instrument are usually underestimating themselves. What happens in practice is that an adult on the right instrument progresses so fast that each week he masters something which was impossible the week before. The continuing achievement provides an automatic source of re-motivation.

The Skill & Motivation Test is an indicator of whether you have the general level of skills and motivation necessary.

| | SCORE NIL | SCORE 10 EACH |
|---|---|---|
| 1. Have you ever pursued a hobby, sporting or leisure interest for more than a few months? | NO | YES |
| 2. Do you have difficulty operating sewing machines, electric drills, typewriters, washing machines? | YES | NO |
| 3. Have you ever played a tune on any instrument, however simple? | NO | YES |
| 4. Have you learnt to drive and passed a Driving Test? | NO | YES |
| 5. Do you admire, or feel jealous of, people you know who can play an instrument, paint, make pottery or have any other creative interest? | NO | YES |
| 6. Would you find it difficult to set aside half an hour each day to practise? | YES | NO |
| 7. Have you said, or thought, many times: "I wish I could play an instrument"? | NO | YES |
| 8. Reading music is easier than mental arithmetic. Can you do the following sums in your head? $99 + 69 =$ $99 - 36 =$ $99 \div 33 =$ $99 \times 3 =$ | NO | YES |
| 9. Do you go out to live entertainment more than twice a year? (If you go regularly to concerts, give yourself a bonus of ten points.) | NO | YES |
| 10. Have you acquired any skill, craft, language, or other body of knowledge since leaving school? | NO | YES |

Score:

To score, multiply by ten the number of times you circled a YES or NO in the right-hand column.

A score of 50 or more indicates the general level of skills and motivation necessary to learn the technically less difficult instruments. A score of 70 or over means that no instrument in this System is too difficult to learn. Sceptics who find that hard to believe are simply confusing the true difficulty of learning an instrument which has been properly and systematically selected with the near-impossibility of trying to learn an unsuitable instrument resulting from a random choice.

If *you* are still unconvinced, there is no need blindly to take our word for it. Instead, think of all the average-ability children who manage to learn instruments designed for your adult body, not their smaller ones. Or, think of the tens of thousands of teenagers, including many a school drop-out, who teach themselves that difficult instrument: the electric guitar. Many of these youngsters could not stitch on a button in the correct place, or drive a car, or do the housekeeping, or perform any of the myriad skills of everyday adult life which you take for granted. As far as learning an instrument is concerned, anything they can do, you can do better—if you want to!

# THE BEN-TOVIM / BOYD SYSTEM:

## PART II: SELECTING YOUR INSTRUMENT

*Use the Summary below as a record of your scores in the Preliminary Tests, placing a tick in the right-hand column against each High Score (70 or over).*

*Note: Suitability of certain instruments involves one or more High Scores.*

|  | Score | High Score |
|---|---|---|
| *RIGHT TIME TEST* |  |  |
| *MUSICALITY TEST* |  |  |
| *SKILL & MOTIVATION TEST* |  |  |

There are two ways of enjoying music: listening and playing. It is strange that they are usually mentioned in that order, for listening is obviously the secondary function. It would be impossible to listen unless someone had made the sound in the first place. Your score in the Musicality Test is an indication of your actual, or latent, ability to *make* music.

There is an instinctive desire to make music within almost everyone. So important and essentially human is this desire that our ancestors sat in Ice Age caves and desert shelters thirty and forty thousand years ago and set time aside from the difficult business of survival in order to make music. That much is known, for pieces of instruments dating back to these times long before the beginning of recorded history have been found and identified.

Even before the first instrument was carved from bone or wood, Mankind had for millennia been humming, singing and whistling. Since such activities leave no trace for us to discover, no one can say for how long men have known the same urge which you feel today—to make music.

The human voice is sometimes called an instrument, but this is inexact and misleading, for an instrument is a tool. Like all tools, it was invented to do something better than we can do with our bodies alone. As the spear and the axe and the hammer were invented to extend the range and power of a man's hand, so musical instruments were invented to extend the range of music beyond what can be achieved with all but the most exceptional human vocal chords.

A musical instrument is a precision tool. It has to be, to fashion something so delicate and precise as music. Learning an instrument is the process of acquiring the skill to operate it well —nothing more mysterious than that.

To appreciate why there is such a thing as the right instrument for a particular person, and conversely others which are wrong, it is necessary first to understand that playing any instrument uses three kinds of energy from the player: physical, mental and emotional. Some instruments take a lot of physical energy and little mental energy; others require much mental and emotional energy, but are physically undemanding.

Some adults have much physical energy unused by modern living, but little or no mental or emotional energy to spare for a new activity. Others have an excess of emotional energy but are physically tired at the end of the working day.

The essence of the Ben-Tovim/Boyd System lies in finding for each individual the instrument which most nearly matches the balance of physical, mental and emotional energy of that individual. In addition, buying, learning and playing the instrument must integrate naturally into the person's normal life-style.

The importance of this Four-Way Matching cannot be overstressed. Every question on the Score Cards, every item on the Information Sheets, is part of the Four-Way Matching Process:

> *physically*, the instrument must suit the body, be comfortable and pleasant to hold and play, but not cause physical stress;
> *mentally*, it must have a technique and repertoire which require just the right amount of mental effort, in order to stimulate but not exhaust;
> *emotionally*, the instrument must make the kind of sound and play the kind of music which express the player's musical personality, in situations where he or she is most happy;
> *in general terms*, buying, learning and playing it must integrate without friction into the other normal activities and commitments of life.

26

The System makes it easy and possible for everyone to do for themselves. All that is necessary, is to read the Information Sheets and fill in the Score Cards. It can be helpful (and amusing) to go through the completed Score Cards with a friend who may "see you very differently from the way you see yourself".

The scoring system functions automatically. Its only purpose is to facilitate comparison of two or more instruments in terms of their suitability for the same person. There is no purpose in comparing one person's scores with another's, nor, in Part II, are there any "pass marks".

For the convenience of composers and conductors, musical instruments are divided into the woodwind, brass, strings and percussion groups. A more helpful way of grouping them, is for the adult would-be player to think in terms of what the instruments offer:

> the ONE-MAN BAND instruments offer musical self-sufficiency to an individual who prefers to make music all alone;

> the JOIN-THE-BAND instruments offer the opportunity to make music with others—in bands, orchestras and other social groups;

> the BEST-OF-BOTH-WORLDS instruments offer the best of both worlds, for they can be played in orchestras, bands and chamber music ensembles, yet can also be pleasurable and satisfying to play on one's own.

# The ONE-MAN-BAND instruments

*". . . offer musical self-sufficiency to the individual who prefers to make music all alone."*

All the orchestral and band instruments (woodwind, brass and strings) were designed to sound one note at a time. In an orchestra or band, chords and harmonies are produced by the simultaneous sounding of several instruments. One of these instruments has comparatively little to offer the music-maker who wishes to be musically self-sufficient and make a complete sound which embraces both melody (the tune) and harmony (the accompaniment).

To make complete music on one's own requires an instrument designed to produce both chords and harmonies. Learning the technique of these instruments, and reading their music, is more difficult than for most of the single-note instruments.

All the instruments in this group are played seated. Playing them demands little physical energy.

High Scores required in:

|  | Piano | Harpsichord Guitar |
|---|---|---|
| *RIGHT TIME TEST* | √ | √ |
| *MUSICALITY TEST* |  | √ |
| *SKILL & MOTIVATION TEST* | √ | √ |

Note: No High Scores required for Electronic Organ

# The Piano

*Information Sheet*

The piano has put more people off music than all the other instruments together. Adults who, as children, suffered weekly lessons for years until eventually eroding the will-power of teacher and parent to the point where release was obtained from this musical torture machine, are numbered in millions. For them even to consider the piano "because I used to have lessons on it", is a waste of time.

On the other hand, those who never had piano lessons and those who progressed beyond the agony stage to some degree of competence, see the piano very differently. For them, the piano can be unequalled as an instrument on which to play alone music from all periods, in all styles. The pianist needs no musical friends. Whenever he feels the need to make music, the completeness of the instrument enables him to sit down and be both conductor and orchestra—literally a one-man band. For singers, there is the added pleasure of accompanying their own voice.

The piano is a highly-developed musical machine which does most of the physical work of producing and pitching the sound. This is important for four reasons:

—there is little or no sensation of playing, or "feedback" into the player's body;
—to operate the instrument requires neither strength nor even health in the player;
—there is no outlet for physical energy in playing the piano;
—a good musical ear is not required.

Reading piano music and translating all those dots into changing hand positions and striking the right keys—up to ten at a time—at the correct moment, is exhilarating if you can do it. If you have the necessary mentality, you will be good at mental arithmetic, the sort of person who can find pleasure in doing several things at the same time. Someone who prefers to concentrate on one thing at a time and finish that before going on to the next, is ill-suited to the piano.

An old-fashioned upright piano seems a large piece of furniture in many modern homes. Those with small rooms prefer the compactness of a modern electric piano, but it is important to get one with a good "feel". Flat-dwellers and learners who prefer the rest of the world not to hear their first efforts enjoy the privacy of playing an electric piano wearing lightweight headphones.

Starting from scratch involves at least two years of hard work. Motivation must be unwavering if the learner is to overcome the periods when no apparent progress is being made. Even a conscientious adult needs a strong relationship with a good teacher.

The eventual reward is competence on the one instrument which enables the player to make virtually every kind of music. There is an easily obtainable repertoire of music for the piano, at all stages of learning.

Method of learning: regular private lessons and daily practice for several years.

# THE PIANO

## *Score Card*

| | SCORE ZERO | SCORE 5 EACH | SCORE 10 EACH |
|---|---|---|---|
| 1. In a supermarket, do you (a) easily keep track of your expenditure, or (b) just guess how much you have spent? | (b) | (a) | |
| 2. Do you enjoy many different kinds of music? | NO | YES | |
| 3. Do you like to organize your day/week/life in advance? | NO | YES | |
| 4. Would you like to set aside a regular practice time each day? | NO | YES | |
| 5. Do you feel it is a long time since you acquired a new skill? | NO | YES | |
| 6. Can you touch-type? | NO | | YES |
| 7. Did you have piano lessons as a child? | NO | YES | |
| 8. Have you previously studied the piano to examination level? | NO | YES | |
| 9. Would you prefer to spend an evening (a) going out with a sociable crowd, or (b) quietly at home with a good book or music to listen to? | (a) | (b) | |
| 10. Would you describe yourself as a conscientious person? | NO | YES | |
| 11. Do you have any nervous or muscular trouble in hands or arms? | YES | NO | |
| 12. Which sound do you prefer: (a) GUITAR or (b) FLUTE? | (b) | (a) | |
| 13. Piano music is difficult to read. Do you see that as (a) A CHALLENGE or (b) A DISCOURAGEMENT? | (b) | (a) | |
| 14. Do you want an instrument on which you can expect quick results? | YES | NO | |

| | (c) | (b) | (a) |
|---|---|---|---|
| 15. Are you (a) ALREADY ABLE TO READ MUSIC, (b) WILLING TO LEARN or (c) NOT INTERESTED IN LEARNING? | (c) | (b) | (a) |
| 16. If you have several conflicting problems at the same time, do you (a) COPE or (b) PANIC? | (b) | | (a) |
| 17. Will you have plenty of spare time in the next couple of years? | NO | YES | |
| 18. Can you name four famous pianists? | NO | YES | |
| 19. Are you willing and able to pay for regular private lessons for the first couple of years at least? | NO | YES | |
| 20. Short-term memory: If you were introduced to six separate strangers at a noisy party, how many of their names would you be likely to remember? | LESS THAN 3 | 3 or 4 | 5 or 6 |

Total of each column:

Score:

*Notes:*

1. *Circle round your answer to each question.*
2. *Make a definite choice between the alternative answers in each case.*
3. *To obtain column totals, multiply by five the number of circled answers in the centre column; multiply by ten the number of circled answers in the right-hand column.*
4. *Add together the two column totals. The result is your Score for Piano.*
5. *The maximum score for each instrument is 120.*
6. *Your Score on the Piano is an indicator of your comparative suitability for this instrument. Enter it on the Scoring Comparison Chart on p. 124.*

# THE CLASSICAL GUITAR

*Information Sheet*

Even among musicians, the guitarist and his instrument are little understood. Many non-players are uncertain about the differences between the classical guitar and the folk and other guitars of the jazz and pop scene. All the other guitars are for improvising, busking, making up your own music or strumming along, possibly using simplified notation, or chord symbols. The classical guitarist reads conventional notation—the music is difficult to read, as the instrument is to play—and plays the full repertoire of serious guitar music.

Although some adults teach themselves classical guitar technique, using one or more of the excellent self-tutor books, almost every learner progresses better and faster by buying private lessons from a teacher, regularly for the first few years, then intermittently for many years to come.

The solitary person who wishes to make complete music alone does not have a great range of instruments to choose from. In order to play both melody (the tune) and harmony (the accompaniment) at the same time, he can use either a keyboard, or the guitar. The keyboards produce the sound mechanically; on the guitar it is the player's body that makes and shapes and controls every aspect of the sound, for the instrument is mechanically the opposite of the piano, being almost as simple in construction as the violin. The simpler the instrument, the more difficult the technique.

The player affects the sound made on a guitar in a thousand ways. Even the composition of the nails, muscle-tone and nervous co-ordination are important. Thus, every guitarist makes a personal sound from the very first scales onwards. The relentless perfectionist finds the long slow mastery of guitar technique endlessly absorbing and increasingly satisfying; the beginner who wants rapid results is swiftly discouraged and gives up.

Whereas playing the keyboards is primarily a cerebral pleasure, playing the guitar is deceptively physical. The volume of sound produced is not large, but the player feels it throughout the body, even resonating in the chest cavity. The keyboards are essentially logical, with each key always producing the same note; guitar logic is more devious, and the same note may be fingered in many

34

ways, depending on the sequence being played. The keyboards can be taken up at almost any age, because the machine does most of the physical work; older people taking up the guitar after fingers have thickened and stiffened and the suppleness gone from wrist and arm, may find it impossible to get a good left hand position, or to do the "stretches". Certainly a sufferer from sciatica or back trouble is unlikely to be comfortable wrapped around a guitar with the left foot raised.

In common with the keyboards, the guitar offers the well-suited player, who has the time for regular lessons and daily practice, an endlessly progressive and inexhaustible repertoire.

Method of learning: regular private lessons, if possible.

# The Classical Guitar

## Score Card

| | SCORE ZERO | SCORE 5 EACH | SCORE 10 EACH |
|---|---|---|---|
| 1. Can you name three classical guitarists? | NO | | YES |
| 2. Which characteristic do you rate more highly: (a) FLAIR or (b) PERSEVERANCE? | (a) | (b) | |
| 3. Do you listen often to guitar music? | NO | YES | |
| 4. Do you ever get back, leg or shoulder pains, e.g. fibrositis, sciatica? | YES | NO | |
| 5. If you find something much more difficult than you had anticipated, do you (a) GIVE UP, (b) TRY A BIT HARDER or (c) BECOME INCREASINGLY DETERMINED TO SUCCEED? | (a) | (b) | (c) |
| 6. Do you enjoy playing chess or cards? | NO | YES | |
| 7. Do you want an instrument to play with others? | YES | NO | |
| 8. Do you have supple fingers and strong nails? | NO | YES | |
| 9. Do you like to organize your day/week/month in advance? | NO | YES | |
| 10. Do you have a good short-term memory? | NO | YES | |
| 11. Do you feel it is time you acquired a new skill? | NO | YES | |
| 12. Have you ever been to a classical guitar recital? | NO | | YES |
| 13. Do you prefer (a) QUICK RESULTS or (b) THE SATISFACTION OF STEADY PROGRESS? | (a) | (b) | |
| 14. Would you, and could you, set aside a regular time for practice each day? | NO | YES | |

|  | SCORE ZERO | SCORE 5 EACH | SCORE 10 EACH |
|---|---|---|---|
| 15. Did you ever learn folk guitar or electric guitar? | NO | YES | |
| 16. Playing the guitar calls for a high degree of finger co-ordination. Have you ever done anything else like this—perhaps making intricate models or doing fine embroidery? | NO | | YES |
| 17. Do you feel that you have never realized your full musical potential? | NO | YES | |
| 18. Did you ever have violin lessons or learn to read music? | NO | YES | |
| 19. Which sound do you prefer: (a) HARP or (b) FLUTE | (b) | (a) | |
| 20. Do you consider yourself an introverted or solitary person? | NO | YES | |

Total of each column:

Score:

*Notes:*

> 1. *To obtain column totals, multiply by five the number of circled answers in the centre column; multiply by ten the number of circled answers in the right-hand column.*
> 2. *Add together the two column totals. The result is your score for the Classical Guitar.*
> 3. *Enter your score in the Scoring Comparison Chart on p. 124.*

# THE HARPSICHORD

*Information Sheet*

"If with the piano you are bored,
Think about the harpsichord."

Not many people seriously consider taking up the harpsichord.
The very idea seems a little eccentric. As the electronic organ said
to the harpsichord: "What's an old-fashioned instrument like you
doing in a modern book like this?"

Twenty years ago, the harpsichord *was* out of fashion. Since
then, the growth in interest in Baroque and early Classical music
has brought a large number of instrument makers into this
market. The result is a wide range of single and two-manual
models, beginning at quite reasonable prices. This delicately
charming instrument is enjoying a new life.

The harpsichord may be just what you are looking for if

—you learnt piano in childhood, or after, passing a few exams;
—you can still read music;
—you remember the logic of the keyboard;
—you enjoy Baroque and early Classical music;
—you are, or a friend is, quite good at tinkering with light
    machines and would quite like the idea of a keyboard
    instrument which the player tunes for himself.

Buying a harpsichord is not difficult. Few music shops keep them
in stock, but music magazines usually have one or two advertisements by makers, who supply ready-made and self-assembly kits.
A visit to their premises is a fascinating experience and also the
best way of picking up some guidance on caring for these
instruments. Current models incorporate some modern materials
in their manufacture and are more reliable than those of tradi-
tional construction, but extremes of temperature and dampness
must be avoided, at risk of warping the instrument.

Method of learning: Occasional lessons from a harpsichordist,
                    possibly combined with a brush-up course
                    on the piano.

## Score Card

| | SCORE ZERO | SCORE 10 EACH |
|---|---|---|
| 1. Which kind of music do you prefer: (a) BAROQUE or EARLY MUSIC, (b) ROMANTIC or MODERN? | (b) | (a) |
| 2. Did you learn to play the piano to approximately Grade V or beyond? | NO | YES |
| 3. Can you name three composers of the Baroque period? | NO | YES |
| 4. Which sound do you prefer: (a) SOLO RECORDER or (b) BRASS BAND? | (b) | (a) |
| 5. The harpsichordist has to tune his instrument regularly. Given instruction, is your ear good enough to do this? | NO | YES |
| 6. Are you a concert-goer, or member of a music club? | NO | YES |
| 7. Do you like the idea of owning or making a harpsichord? | NO | YES |
| 8. Did you get a high score on the piano? | NO | YES |
| 9. Do you feel that your musical interests have failed to develop over the last few years and that it is time to expand them by doing something active and different? | NO | YES |
| 10. Are you conscientious enough to look after an instrument which requires regular care? | NO | YES |
| 11. Should the "new instrument in your life" be one to play (a) AT HOME/IN SMALL CHAMBER GROUPS or (b) IN ORCHESTRAS OR LARGE GROUPS? | (b) | (a) |
| 12. Are you attracted by the sound of the harpsichord? | NO | YES |
| Score: | | |

# THE ELECTRONIC ORGAN

## Information Sheet

The piano is a triumph of nineteenth-century mechanical engineering. It reduces to the minimum the *physical* work of making complete and self-contained music. The electronic organ, or home organ, is a twentieth-century up-dating of the same idea: to the logic of the keyboard has been added all the tricks of solid-state circuitry, reducing to a minimum the physical and the mental work of playing both melody and harmony at the same time.

The home organ is not an 'easier piano'. It does not provide the same rewards and satisfactions as the mechanical keyboard. It is a miracle of today's technology and marketing designed to meet the musical needs of two kinds of people. The first are those who want the feeling of playing with others, but, for one reason or another, cannot actually get out and join a group. The second are people who are naturally outgoing and sociable and would join a group of some kind in order to make music in a social situation, if only their normal working day did not use up all their "social energy". Examples of the second group are sales reps, bank cashiers, doctors, nurses, receptionists. Both groups use the electronic organ to have the feeling of playing with others, whenever they want it, at the touch of a switch.

The organ is an undemanding electronic friend. It provides, on command, rhythms, harmonies, even the synthetic sound of whole orchestral sections. Any player who can pick out a tune by ear, or read a simple tune, can be backed if not by heavenly choirs, at least by electronic choruses.

Perhaps those who get the most out of these instruments are today's equivalent of the natural, untaught amateur musician who used to tinkle on the piano, producing from ear and memory songs from the shows, classical bits and pieces and the latest popular music.

Owners often take advantage of manufacturers' simplified notation and learn rapidly to play a restricted number of tunes, playing about with the backing as the mood takes them. There is a danger of losing heart on the part of the owner who cannot play be ear and gest bored with this small repertoire, for his only alternative is to learn to read conventional notation through a course of formal lessons. The organ-owner who can read music properly has access to a lifetime's repertoire of keyboard music.

Method of learning: Initially by self-tutor book and/or show-room group lessons.
Individual private lessons are necessary for sustained progress.

# THE ELECTRONIC ORGAN

## Score Card

| | SCORE ZERO | SCORE 5 EACH |
|---|---|---|
| 1. Do you enjoy owning and looking after good-quality possessions? | NO | YES |
| 2. Would you like an instrument that makes you sound "as good as a pro" straight away? | NO | YES |
| 3. Have you always been able to pick out a tune on piano or some other instrument? | NO | YES |
| 4. Would you like the feeling of playing with a band or orchestra, yet find it impossible to join a group, due to your life-style? | NO | YES |
| 5. Do you feel that you could have been quite good on the piano, but have left it too late to start all that work now? | NO | YES |
| 6. Have you had many different hobbies and/or sports interests throughout your life? | NO | YES |
| 7. Are you good at making or mending things in the home? | NO | YES |
| 8. Can you read music? | NO | YES |
| 9. Do you have a natural sense of harmony, i.e. do you just know when things sound right together? | NO | YES |
| 10. Which kind of sound do you prefer: (a) SOLO GUITAR or (b) A WHOLE BAND | (a) | (b) |
| 11. Are you (a) NEAT & TIDY or (b) RATHER MESSY & DISORGANIZED? | (b) | (a) |
| 12. Do you want an instrument to play (a) SEATED or (b) STANDING? | (b) | (a) |
| 13. If you had sufficient money, would you (a) change your car each year for a new model, or (b) save? | (b) | (a) |
| 14. Do you prefer Classical to swing-ey or pop music? | YES | NO |
| 15. Do you really enjoy the sound of electronic organs? | NO | YES |
| 16. At a social gathering, would you like to be able to play a few numbers? | NO | YES |

| | | |
|---|---|---|
| 17. Are you prepared to spend several hundred pounds on an instrument? | NO | YES |
| 18. Are you the sort of person who might have plenty of time to practise one week, and none the next? | NO | YES |
| 19. Are you looking for an instrument on which you will rapidly be able to express your personality? | NO | YES |
| 20. Which do you prefer: (a) THE SATISFACTION OF STEADY PROGRESS or (b) THE EXCITEMENT OF RAPID RESULTS? | (a) | (b) |
| 21. Do you enjoy using and operating complicated machines? | NO | YES |
| 22. Have you ever learnt the piano? | NO | YES |
| 23. Do you fancy the idea of an instrument on which you can play around, achieving different effects? | NO | YES |
| 24. Are you good at telling funny stories? | NO | YES |
| Score: | | |

## The JOIN-THE-BAND instruments

"... offer the opportunity to make music with others—in bands, orchestras and other social groups."

Each band or orchestral instrument produces only one note at a time, or supplies rhythm. Learning a single-note instrument to the level of playing in amateur bands or orchestras can be rapid. On some of these instruments, the well-suited adult can expect to begin playing a few notes in a band within a few weeks of starting to learn.

If playing your heart out in a musical team is your idea of making music, one of this group of instruments can lead to a radical enrichment of social life by joining one—or more than one—of these musical clubs, enjoying regular companionship at weekly rehearsals, performing in concerts, taking part in competitions and so on.

High Scores required in:

|  | Drumkit Saxophone | Orchestral Double Bass | Trombone | Trumpet Baritone Cornet Orchestral | Euphonium Tenor Horn Tuba Percussion |
|---|---|---|---|---|---|
| *RIGHT TIME TEST* |  |  |  |  |  |
| *MUSICALITY TEST* |  | √ | √ | √ | √ |
| *SKILL & MOTIVATION TEST* | √ | √ |  |  |  |

# THE BRASS INSTRUMENTS

*Information Sheet*

Some people are not attracted to the almost choral quality of brass band music and therefore overlook that this group of instruments has a lot to offer any adult who wants to make music with others, scores well in the Musicality Test and is reasonably fit and energetic. One or more brass instruments appear on most Short Lists.

All these instruments are variations on the simple horn: a mouthpiece connected to a tube. The player purses his lips and blows a raspberry against the mouthpiece. The air in the tube amplifies and modulates the sound. That looks an unlikely way of making music, when written down, but it works. To produce the whole range of notes requires a combination of a number of lip-positions with use of the three valves by co-ordinated use of three fingers of the right hand—except on the trombone, which is the odd man out, having a slide instead of valves.

A good sense of pitch is needed, because the mechanics of the instruments are simple, with any position of the valves producing several notes. So, the player monitors his own and the group sound the whole time he is playing. The process sounds complicated, but comes naturally to most people, because the actual operation of the instrument is so simple.

The feeling of playing brass has been likened to singing one's heart out in a choir and having a good work-out in the gym at the same time, but some people do not like pushing gently with the belly muscles and vibrating the lips against the mouthpiece, which puts their teeth on edge. If you are one of these people, there is no way you could enjoy playing a brass instrument.

The lover of Classical music, who wants to play in an orchestra, has a choice of three instruments: trumpet, trombone and tuba (the French Horn is dealt with elsewhere). Brass band fans have a much wider choice of instruments: everything *except* the trumpet. If you want to make jazz, or play in dance bands or big bands, you cannot overlook trumpet and trombone. Trumpet, trombone and tuba are also used in chamber music.

The average brass band is the friendliest musical "club" you could hope to join. New members of either sex are always welcome, no matter what their age, previous musical experience

46

or lack of it. The band will lend you an instrument to learn, and technique is usually picked up from other members of the section at weekly band practice sessions.

Because of the basic similarity of all the instruments in this group, it is possible to simplify the individual Score Cards and make the Information Sheets more useful by first evaluating your overall potential for brass instruments generally. If your Brass rating is positive, you add a bonus to your score for each instrument. If it is negative, you treat that as a handicap and deduct it from each score.

*As all these instruments have so much in common, it is useful to measure the general suitability of the Brass for you, before considering each individual instrument. Use the Score Card over-leaf to determine your Brass Instruments Rating.*

# BRASS INSTRUMENTS RATING

| | SCORE −5 EACH | SCORE ZERO | SCORE +5 EACH |
|---|---|---|---|
| 1. Do you often whistle to yourself when alone, or concentrating? | | NO | YES |
| 2. Would you enjoy spending the evening in a crowded pub with a group of noisy friends? | NO | | YES |
| 3. Do you (a) ALWAYS FEEL TIRED AT THE END OF THE DAY or (b) USUALLY HAVE PLENTY OF SPARE PHYSICAL ENERGY? | (a) | | (b) |
| 4. Did you ever play bugle or other brass instrument, e.g. in a cadet band, Scouts? | | NO | YES |
| 5. Would you describe yourself as (a) A LONER or (b) QUIETLY SOCIABLE or (c) A TEAM PERSON? | (a) | (b) | (c) |
| 6. Have you lost any of your natural front teeth, or do you suffer from any gum troubles? | YES | NO | |
| 7. If you blow a raspberry against the back of your hand, do you (a) LIKE or (b) DISLIKE the feeling? | (b) | | (a) |
| 8. Do you instinctively join in, when others start singing at a sporting event or social evening? | NO | YES | |
| 9. Do you suffer from any of the following: HERNIA / PILES / RESPIRATORY TROUBLE? | YES | NO | |
| 10. Are you usually tense or obsessive? | YES | NO | |
| Total of each column: | − | ZERO | + |

Your Brass Rating:

*Notes:*
*Your Brass Rating may be positive or negative. To find it, score as follows:*

 *1. Multiply by five the numbers of circled answers in the left and right-hand columns. Enter the total at the bottom of each column.*

 *2. The left total is negative, e.g. three circles in the left column give a total of −15.*

 *3. The right total is positive, e.g. four circles in the right column give a total of +20.*

 *4. Your Brass rating is obtained by combining the two column totals, subtracting the lesser from the greater.*
 *e.g. −15 and +20 give a Rating of +5*
 *but −25 and +10 give a Rating of −15, and so on.*

*You will need to add or subtract your Brass Rating when scoring each individual brass instrument.*

# THE TRUMPET

## Information Sheet

More non-players think of taking up the trumpet than any other brass instrument, but this is only because the trumpet, being powerful and high-sounding, is the instrument most often heard in the composite sound of a band. Many bandleaders are former trumpeters, so their personal fame has attracted people to the instrument. Most people could name a couple of trumpeters, but would have difficulty in remembering even one oboeist or euphonium-player.

What makes a trumpeter? He must be very fit, have endless, even restless, energy and drive. He needs perfect teeth and healthy gums. He also requires a first-class sense of pitch, to hit his notes without fumbling; if he fumbles, everyone hears. Not an instrument for the shy or retiring, the trumpet most rewards the player who wants to dominate or lead the group. The kind of physical energy required is the short-burst fire of a sprinter, rather than the stamina of the long- or middle-distance runner.

A good amateur trumpeter may play in several different kinds of musical group each week. He is welcome in orchestras, all bands (except brass bands, where the lead parts are played on cornet) and in chamber groups. Those whose satisfaction lies in playing written music immaculately move towards amateur orchestras, while others who seek the freedom to express themselves in improvising, head for the jazz scene. In big bands and dance bands, the trumpeter must be able to do both kinds of playing.

Most trumpeters have some individual private lessons, often regularly for the first couple of years. While many other brass-players of amateur standard practise only at the weekly band rehearsal, the trumpeter must practise each day, in order to "keep his lip in". On the other hand if he plays too·much, he risks "losing his lip". The difference between a good and bad embouchure on the trumpet is glaringly obvious. A trumpeter is a natural risk-taker.

Social opportunities: Symphony, opera, chamber orchestras and groups. Military, dance, concert and big bands. Jazz.

Method of learning: Regular private lessons recommended at first.

## Score Card

| | SCORE ZERO | SCORE 5 EACH | SCORE 10 EACH |
|---|---|---|---|
| 1. Do you have far more energy than most of your colleagues or acquaintances? | NO | | YES |
| 2. In a group of people, would it feel natural to dominate or hog the limelight? | NO | | YES |
| 3. Are you (a) AMBITIOUS or (b) EASY-GOING? | (b) | (a) | |
| 4. Do you like many different kinds of music? | NO | YES | |
| 5. Is your voice (a) NORMAL/HIGH or (b) RATHER LOW? | (b) | (a) | |
| 6. Are you (a) a risk-taker or (b) naturally cautious? | (b) | | (a) |
| 7. Have you a fine sense of pitch? | NO | | YES |
| 8. Have you perfect teeth and gums? | NO | | YES |
| 9. Do you want an instrument on which you can express your personality? | NO | YES | |
| 10. Are you troubled by headaches or sinusitis? | YES | NO | |
| 11. Have you ever learnt to play any brass instrument? | NO | YES | |
| 12. Can you name three or more famous trumpeters? | NO | | YES |

Total of each column:

Combined total:

*Add/Subtract your Brass Rating:

Score:

*If you had a positive Rating, add it. If your Rating was negative, subtract it.

# THE CORNET

## Information Sheet

The cornet is the basic instrument of the brass (and silver) band. Although it may look like some kind of chubby trumpet, it is a different instrument, far easier to learn and to play. The initial stage of learning is rapid. Most adults who like the feedback of playing brass could begin playing cornet in a brass band after two or three weeks' practice at home with a self-tutor book.

People who do not know about brass bands are incredulous at first, and then delighted when they realize that it is quite normal for beginners to sit in the second cornet section, contributing only the notes they know so far. Gradually, they pick up more and more technique from the other members of the section. Some practice at home is needed in the initial period. Played with a mute, the cornet does not make too much noise, even for a flat-dweller. The basic quality of sound is pleasant, so the beginner is not discouraged.

The only big drawback of the cornet is that, if you live in an area with no brass bands, there is nowhere to play it. If you do have a local band, you will find that the cornet sections include many easy-going players who practise very little and are content to carry on playing the simpler parts. The more ambitious work up their technique between band sessions, while those few who have a good lip and like living dangerously can rise rapidly through the sections to become Solo Cornet. This takes the same kind of nerve as playing the trumpet. In a brass band, the Solo Cornet is the star of the show—a bit like the Leader in an orchestra.

If you are thinking about the brass and are uncertain about any particular instrument, there is a lot to be said for taking up the cornet initially. You can always transfer later on, and in the meantime will have acquired basic brass technique, "got your lip in" and have begun training your ear as well. Even if you can't see yourself playing in brass bands long-term, a few months learning the cornet can work miracles for any adult who suffered a musical accident. This is a most effective way of re-building one's damaged musical self-confidence.

All the players in brass bands must read music, but the parts are not difficult to read, since the instruments play only one note at a time. Few of the members can read music when they first join, but all just pick it up as they go along, with help from their neighbours. Even those with a block about reading music dating from childhood piano or school music lessons find this a painless way of becoming musically literate.

Social opportunities: Brass bands. Military bands.
Method of learning:  Self-tutor books. Help from other players. Occasional lessons for advanced technique.

# THE CORNET

## Score Card

| | SCORE ZERO | SCORE 5 EACH | SCORE 10 EACH |
|---|---|---|---|
| 1. Do you habitually (a) WHISTLE or (b) SING favourite tunes? | NO | (b) | (a) |
| 2. Would you like to be able to join a band within a couple of weeks? | NO | YES | |
| 3. Is your voice (a) LOW or (b) MIDDLE/HIGH? | (a) | | (b) |
| 4. Would you say you are SLOW BUT SURE, rather than RISKY AND FAST? | NO | YES | |
| 5. Would you most enjoy listening to (a) BRASS BAND (b) DANCE BAND or (c) ORCHESTRA? | (c) | (b) | (a) |
| 6. Do you belong to one or more sporting or social clubs? | NO | YES | |
| 7. Would you enjoy the regular attendance at weekly band practice, and eventually playing in weekend and evening concerts? | NO | | YES |
| 8. Do you want to make steady progress with a reasonable minimum of practice? | NO | YES | |
| 9. Very few cornettists ever hear themselves play a solo. They contribute to the joint sound of the section. Does this attract you, or not? | NO | | YES |
| 10. Are your lips (a) THICK or (b) THIN/AVERAGE? | (a) | (b) | |

11. Once in a band, the cornettist has a choice: he can stay on the easy parts or he can work to improve his technique and move to more difficult ones. Does this choice attract you?

12. Which sound do you prefer: (a) VIOLIN or (b) BASSOON?

| | NO | YES |
|---|---|---|
| | (b) | (a) |

Total of each column:

Combined total:
Add/Subtract your Brass Rating:
Score:

# Tenor Horn, Baritone & Euphonium

## Information Sheet

As a choir is made up of some high, some low and some middle voices, so a brass band is made up of high instruments (the cornets), the low ones (basses) and the middle-sounding ones: tenor horns, baritones and euphoniums. The sound made by all these middle horns is mellow and pleasant. Never a harsh note between them!

Adults who do not understand much about music—and children—tend to hear only the top of a composite sound, and the rhythms. Treble instruments may have most of the tunes and be better-known, but the middle instruments of any group are very important, too; they supply most of the harmony or colour. A dominant person, or one who likes being in the limelight, would find them unrewarding. They are mostly played by good-natured, responsive people who like working with others and don't really want to be singled out for praise or blame.

That does not mean that middle-horn players are nonentities. They may be undemanding, but they are naturally conscientious people, often taking on the administrative side of the band, acting as librarians, band secretaries, organizing travel schedules to "away" concerts and festivals, etc.

To look at, the tenor horns and baritones are baby tubas, but their size, shape and weight makes them comfortable and easy to hold and play. They require very little puff. In mixed bands (most of them are today), there are more women in these sections than among the cornets or basses. Technique is easy to acquire, particularly if you have done a few months on cornet. Very few players ever buy their instruments, which are simply borrowed from the band. Some players never practise at home; some practise a little between rehearsals.

The euphonium (the name means "sweet-sounding") is a small-size tuba, but still not a bass instrument. Players usually move on to it after starting on cornet or other horns—at the suggestion of the band organizers. Euphonium-players occasionally have a tune and variations to play on their own but spend the rest of their time enriching the harmonies, like the other horns.

Social opportunities: Brass bands. Euphonium also in military bands.

Method of learning: No formal lessons, but a lot of help from other players.

## Score Card

| | SCORE ZERO | SCORE 5 EACH | SCORE 10 EACH |
|---|---|---|---|
| 1. Do you like brass band music? | NO | | YES |
| 2. Are you the kind of person who makes a popular, not bossy, organizer? | NO | YES | |
| 3. Is your voice (a) HIGH, (b) MIDDLE or (c) LOW? | (a) | (c) | (b) |
| 4. Have you ever enjoyed singing in a choir? | NO | | YES |
| 5. These instruments rarely play tunes. Would you find this frustrating? | YES | | NO |
| 6. Do you easily get bored? | YES | NO | |
| 7. Do you have many friends? | NO | YES | |
| 8. Do you resent "being told what to do"? | YES | | NO |
| 9. Are your lips (a) THIN or (b) AVERAGE TO GENEROUS? | (a) | (b) | |
| 10. Are you interested in learning an instrument which only plays in brass bands? | NO | | YES |
| 11. Do you prefer (a) WORKING UNDER PRESSURE or (b) TAKING YOUR TIME ABOUT THINGS? | (a) | (b) | |
| 12. Would you be prepared to learn one of these instruments to help out the band, if there were a shortage of players? | NO | YES | |

Total of each column:

Combined total:
Add/Subtract your Brass Rating:
Total Score:

57

# The Tuba or E Flat / B Flat Bass

*Information Sheet*

Question: What's the difference between a tuba and an E Flat (or B Flat) bass?
Answer: None.

The largest and lowest-sounding of the brass instruments is called a tuba in the orchestra and a bass in the brass band. An orchestra has one tuba-player, which makes life rather lonely, but in a band, there is a whole bass section.

One of the reasons why people like the sound of particular instruments is that they *hear* these instruments better than others. This usually has to do with the register of their own voices. That is not as crazy as it sounds, for our ears are naturally tuned to hear the sound we make ourselves. Thus, people with higher-pitched voices tend to get more enjoyment from the sound of treble instruments while those with middle-register voices prefer the middle register instruments. Many people who are attracted to the bass instruments have middle-to-low voices; very few have high voices.

Whether you use the orchestral or the band name for them, these instruments are BIG! Too big to carry around, so most players leave them where the band rehearses, if necessary having another instrument at home for practice. Holding and playing the instrument is really only comfortable for someone on the large side, but the effort of playing the tuba is far less than one would think: you don't have to fill all that tube with air from your lungs for each note; it is the other way round, for the air in the tube acts as an amplifier—like the old-fashioned gramophone horn.

Most tuba-players began their playing on cornet and/or one of the middle horns, moving on to the tuba because they found its sound more satisfying. You need a sense of humour to play these giants of the brass world.

These instruments are self-selecting. Few people want to play them, but those who do, know. The point of the Score Card for most is a negative one; but it gives you a standard of comparison for your other brass instrument Score Cards.

Social opportunities: Orchestra. Brass bands. Concert and military bands. Brass chamber groups.

Method of learning: Regular lessons for orchestral playing; occasional lessons for band.

## Score Card

| | SCORE ZERO | SCORE 5 EACH | SCORE 10 EACH |
|---|---|---|---|
| 1. Would you be physically comfortable playing such a large, bulky instrument? | NO | | YES |
| 2. If made manager of a club or band, would you be flexible and tolerant? | NO | YES | |
| 3. Have you ever sung bass parts, or played piano or any bass instrument? | NO | | YES |
| 4. Are your lips (a) THIN/AVERAGE or (b) GENEROUS? | (a) | | (b) |
| 5. Are you physically strong and healthy? | NO | YES | |
| 6. In team games, would you be placed (a) IN DEFENCE or (b) ATTACKER? | (b) | (a) | |
| 7. Can you laugh at a joke against yourself? | NO | YES | |
| 8. Do you have a natural sense of rhythm, "conducting" or tapping a foot whenever you hear music? | NO | YES | |
| 9. Do you weigh (a) LESS THAN AVERAGE FOR YOUR HEIGHT or (b) MORE? | (a) | (b) | |
| 10. Is your voice (a) HIGH/MIDDLE or (b) LOW? | (a) | | (b) |
| 11. Have you previously learnt another brass instrument? | NO | | YES |
| 12. Had the idea of playing the tuba ever occurred to you, before reading this book? | NO | | YES |

Total of each column:

Combined total:
Add/Subtract your Brass Rating:
Score:

# THE TROMBONE

## Information Sheet

The trombone is the most difficult instrument to learn in this group.

Mechanically, it is extremely simple: no valves or other bits and pieces to help the player, just a mouthpiece and tube which he lengthens and shortens, guided by the evidence of his own ears. All the work of producing the sound is done by the player, who thus has the satisfaction of controlling his sound as much as any guitarist or violinist.

Even to play a series of oompahs, the trombonist can never relax, because he must monitor each note and adjust his lips and his instrument minutely while he is playing it. To make a good trombonist, you need to be alert and agile mentally as well as fit and well-co-ordinated physically. The sort of physique that does well at cricket, skating, dancing is typical of trombonists.

Only one thing is easier on the trombone than on the other brass: finger-control. You don't use any fingers individually, of course. Would-be trombonists get off to a better start if they have sung in a choir, can read music or have previously gained basic brass lip technique on the cornet or any other brass instrument. Women who have sung alto parts and men tenors are naturals for the trombone.

The trombone plays in more different situations than any other brass instrument, so if you have a good Brass Rating and like the feedback of playing brass, yet do not want to be limited to any one kind of music, think of the trombone. It is hard work to learn, even with regular lessons and plenty of practice between them, but the rewards are commensurate: a satisfying and very music-ally expressive instrument to play and the widest possible range of music and social opportunities.

The trombonist never needs to get bored. He can play anony-mously in military or brass band section, change to Classical music in an orchestra (where he may be asked to read music in three different clefs), indulge his need for musical self-expression in a jazz band, let rip with a big band, go all serious in an introspective brass chamber group—even go down the pit, not as a miner, but to play for amateur operatics or musicals. And he may well enjoy all these kinds of playing equally as a therapy for his restless intelligence.

Social opportunities: Brass and military bands. Big bands. Dance bands. Jazz. Symphony, chamber and opera orchestras. Chamber groups.
Method of learning: Regular lessons advisable.

## Score Card

| | SCORE ZERO | SCORE 5 EACH | SCORE 10 EACH |
|---|---|---|---|
| 1. Do you feel that you are an artistic or creative person, even though you may not have found a way of expressing this until now? | NO | | YES |
| 2. Are your arms (a) SHORT, (b) MEDIUM or (c) LONG? | (a) | (b) | (c) |
| 3. Would you like to play many different kinds of music? | NO | YES | |
| 4. Are you a good all-rounder? | NO | YES | |
| 5. Have you done athletics, skating, gymnastics, dancing or any similar physical activity? | NO | | YES |
| 6. Do you have a very good musical ear? | NO | | YES |
| 7. Are you reasonably fit and agile? | NO | YES | |
| 8. Do you easily get bored? | NO | YES | |
| 9. Are you (a) OVERWEIGHT or (b) SLIM TO AVERAGE BUILD? | (a) | (b) | |
| 10. Have you sung written parts in a choir or otherwise learned to read music? | NO | | YES |
| 11. Is your voice (a) LOW OR HIGH or (b) MIDDLE-RANGE? | (a) | (b) | |
| 12. Would you describe yourself as witty? | NO | | YES |

Total of each column:

Combined total:
Add/Subtract your Brass Rating:
Total Score:

# THE SAXOPHONE

## Information Sheet

The saxophone is a fun instrument for jazz and light music. If you enjoy the sounds of Mancini or the MJQ and would never listen to Mozart from choice, think of the sax. It tells you something about the instrument that it is hardly ever called by its full name. In every sense, it is an informal instrument, never stuffy or pompous.

There are two characteristics you either like or don't. The first is the unmistakable throaty, almost hoarse voice of the sax and the second is the large mouthpiece which is placed inside the lips. The vibration of the reed is quite strong, yet some people who don't like the brass feedback can happily play sax for hours without being disturbed by it.

At first sight, all that shiny keywork on the outside of the sax can be off-putting. Actually, the complicated mechanics are the reason why the instrument is so easy to play. You need generous lips and good strong front teeth to play the sax, which weighs quite a lot. The sling around the player's neck takes some of the strain, but if you have pains in or trouble with neck, shoulders or back, you may find the twisted position of playing the instrument, and the weight, uncomfortable.

The combination of the reed, the woodwind-type keywork and the resonant quality of brass makes the sax quite efficient acoustically, but playing it does release pent-up physical energy, which is important for anyone who spends too long in an office chair or behind a steering wheel.

If you could ever play a few tunes on the recorder, or began flute or oboe and gave up, you already have a flying start on the sax which uses the same basic fingering. It helps if you can read music, but that is not vital because the music is easy to read.

There are many good self-tutor books for alto sax. This is the first one to learn: changing to soprano, baritone or tenor sax is easy. Progress is exhilaratingly fast for most people, but occasionally lessons can be taken from local pro and semi-pro players to speed things up or get over a particular problem.

Of all the woodwind instruments, the sax suits people with a strong sense of rhythm—perhaps betrayed by habitually tapping steering wheel or desk, or compulsive foot-tapping.

There is one rather crafty reason for taking up the sax. If you want within a reasonable time to be playing with a local jazz or light music band, you will find a lot of competition on trumpet, flute, trombone etc. On the sax, there is less, because it is not such an obvious choice, so you will have a better chance of getting playing experience than on another instrument you might play equally well.

Social opportunities: Jazz, dance and big bands. Military bands. Almost any light music combination.
Method of learning:  Self-tutor books. Occasional lessons.

# The Saxophone

## Score Card

| | SCORE ZERO | SCORE 5 EACH | SCORE 10 EACH |
|---|---|---|---|
| 1. Would you be satisfied by an instrument which is quick to learn and fun to play? | NO | | YES |
| 2. In a group of instruments, would you instantly recognize the throaty sound of the sax? | NO | YES | |
| 3. Do you have a collection of light music or jazz on record or cassette? | NO | YES | |
| 4. Would your friends describe you as casual, easy-going? | NO | YES | |
| 5. Would you prefer (a) AN INSTRUMENT WHICH IS LEARNT WITHOUT LESSONS FROM A PROPER TEACHER or (b) ONE FOR WHICH YOU HAVE REGULAR LESSONS? | (b) | (a) | |
| 6. A saxophone mouthpiece is quite large and the reed vibrates inside the mouth. Do you think this would bother you? | YES | | NO |
| 7. The sax is good for improvising. Does that idea appeal to you? | NO | YES | |
| 8. Do you want to play light music and/or jazz? | NO | | YES |
| 9. Are your lips (a) THIN, (b) AVERAGE or (c) THICK? | (a) | (b) | (c) |
| 10. Do you react strongly to rhythmic music, e.g. by clicking fingers, tapping a foot, etc? | NO | | YES |

11. Are you free from back
trouble, and do you have strong
front teeth, with healthy gums?
12. Did you ever learn recorder or
any other woodwind instrument?
        Total of each column:

        Combined total:
        Add/Subtract your Woodwind Rating:
        Score:

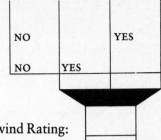

*Because the sax is a woodwind instrument—the only one in this
group—you will need to add or subtract your Woodwind Rating
to your score. Don't worry about this. Fill in the Score Card now
and enter the Rating later.*

# THE ORCHESTRAL DOUBLE BASS

*Information Sheet*

The orchestral double bass may strike you as one of the less likely instruments in this book, but it is worthy of serious consideration by quite a lot of music-lovers, particularly if they

—ever learnt any stringed instrument and did reasonably well,
—can read bass clef,
—enjoy orchestral, especially Classical, music,
—are physically big enough to be comfortable on this large instrument,
—have rather large hands with a wide span and fingers which are long and strong but perhaps feel clumsy on smaller instruments.

Most amateur orchestras are always on the lookout for bass-players, partly because it is not an obvious instrument for an adult to take up and partly because instruments are expensive and not easy to come by. Because basses are fragile for their size, they get easily damaged. Most amateur and pro players have old, much-repaired instruments which make a good quality of sound. Sound quality is very important to bassists; they feel the sound they are making through their bellies, literally. Few in the audience, nor even most conductors, can pick out the individual sound of a particular bassist in the section, but the bass-players feel their music more strongly than most of the other members of the orchestra, because their giant instruments are natural amplifiers sending vibration throughout their bodies.

Unlike the bass in pop or rock music, the orchestral bass is primarily harmonic, like the basses in a choir. To play a bass instrument harmonically requires a good musical ear. To play any string instrument takes an excellent sense of pitch. To play double bass in an orchestra, you need to be a very musical person.

Many thousands of people had rather unsatisfactory violin lessons in childhood. They think they have forgotten everything they ever learned about string technique, yet find that the bass "begins to click" after a few months of learning. There are no overnight results, but progress can be very fast, and the adult learner be ready for an orchestra within the year. For the passionate lover of Classical music, there are fewer greater pleasures than being able to play in an orchestra.

Social opportunities: Symphony, opera and chamber orchestra.
Bands. Jazz and folk music.
Method of learning: Regular lessons to acquire basic technique.

# The Orchestral Double Bass

## Score Card

| | SCORE ZERO | SCORE 5 EACH | SCORE 10 EACH |
|---|---|---|---|
| 1. Are you (a) TALL or (b) AVERAGE HEIGHT OR LESS? | (b) | | (a) |
| 2. When listening to an orchestra all playing together, can you easily hear what the basses are doing? | NO | | YES |
| 3. Do you have a wide hand-span and long, strong fingers? | NO | | YES |
| 4. Is your voice (a) LOW, (b) MEDIUM or (c) HIGH? | (c) | (b) | (a) |
| 5. Do you have a good sense of rhythm? | NO | YES | |
| 6. Can you read bass clef? | NO | YES | |
| 7. The double bass is about six feet high. Would you be prepared to change car, if necessary, to transport a bass? | NO | | YES |
| 8. When in a group of people, do you want to dominate? | YES | NO | |
| 9. Do you get unaccountably depressed from time to time? | NO | YES | |
| 10. Are you (a) IMPATIENT or (b) PATIENT? | (a) | (b) | |
| 11. Have you a very good musical ear, or sung bass in a choir? | NO | YES | |
| 12. Can you see yourself playing the double bass? | NO | | YES |
| Total of each column: | | | |

Combined total:
Add/Subtract your Strings Rating:
Total Score:

*The bass is the only stringed instrument in this group. You will need to add/subtract your Strings Rating to your score. Don't worry about this. Fill in the Score Card now and enter the Rating later.*

# THE ORCHESTRAL PERCUSSION

## Information Sheet

There is one very quick way of joining the band—or, more probably, an orchestra—which is open to anyone who had piano lessons to the level of taking a few exams. If the piano was chosen for you by a parent and you are not naturally a solitary person, all the progress you made was the result of sheer hard work. Quite logically, you have little reason to wish to "go through all that again" by starting to learn another instrument from scratch. Yet, the solitary pleasure of the piano is not what you need, to satisfy your musical appetites.

Or, perhaps you quite enjoy playing the piano, but would like to make music with other like-minded people. If your piano-playing is not up to chamber music standard, what can you do?

In either case, you are admirably equipped with no further training to join the percussion section of an amateur orchestra, concert band or military band. The music is unbelievably easy to read compared to piano music, and your piano training has given you an understanding of basic percussion technique.

In an orchestra, the percussion section is a self-contained, self-organizing club. All the players are sensitive, meticulous people. Their kind of playing is a far cry from bashing everything in sight on a rock drumkit. The exact placing of a triangle beat or trill on the tambourine takes more skill—and is far more satis-fying—than concert-goers realize.

Usually, each percussionist plays several instruments in each piece of music, standing, not seated as at the piano. Side drum and timpani are the two specialist areas rarely begun by adults. The tuned percussion are all based on the same keyboard logic as the piano, so the ex-pianist has the whole range of the other instruments to play with.

The un-tuned percussion are also open to anyone who learned to play any instrument and can read music. Examples are clarinet-tists and oboeists who have lost teeth, or the strings player who is not quite good enough to get into the strings sections, and so on.

However unlikely it seems, if you score highly in this test, it is worth a visit and a chat with your local orchestra. They may well be looking for someone just like you.

Social opportunities: Symphony and opera orchestras. Concert and military bands.

Method of learning: Help from other players, plus occasional lessons, added to previous musical experience.

# THE ORCHESTRAL PERCUSSION

## Score Card

| | SCORE ZERO | SCORE 5 EACH | SCORE 10 EACH |
|---|---|---|---|
| 1. Would you like to join an amateur orchestra, but feel ineligible for brass, woodwind or strings sections? | NO | | YES |
| 2. Do you think that playing music has to be a way of expressing your personality? | YES | NO | |
| 3. In your personal habits, are you (a) NEAT & TIDY (b) MIDDLING (c) MESSY & UNTIDY? | (c) | (b) | (a) |
| 4. Did you study piano to above Grade III? (Score 5 if you studied some other instrument to examination level.) | NO | OTHER | YES |
| 5. Can you read music easily? | NO | YES | |
| 6. Are you good with your hands, able to make and mend things in the home? | NO | YES | |
| 7. When a child, were you thought of, or labelled, HYPERACTIVE? | NO | YES | |
| 8. A percussion player spends a great deal of time "counting bars' rest". Could you do this? (a) YES (b) NO or DON'T KNOW | (b) | | (a) |
| 9. Would you be happy to work in a small team? | NO | YES | |
| 10. Do you prefer (a) TO WORK STEADILY AWAY AT ONE THING or (b) TO CHOP & CHANGE? | (a) | (b) | |
| 11. Do you willingly accept necessary discipline? | NO | YES | |
| 12. Do you regularly sleep (a) MORE or (b) LESS than seven hours a night? | (a) | (b) | |
| 13. Are you interested in theory of music, or have you ever taken a theory exam? | NO | YES | |

| | | |
|---|---|---|
| 14. Which personal characteristic do you rate more highly in others: (a) FLAIR or (b) ACCURACY? | (a) | (b) |
| 15. Is your physical build (a) THIN/AVERAGE or (b) LARGE/OVERWEIGHT? | (b) | (a) |
| 16. Which sound do you prefer: (a) FLUTE or (b) GUITAR? | (a) | (b) |
| 17. Would you prefer an instrument played (a) SEATED or (b) STANDING | (a) | (b) |
| 18. Do you have a better than average sense of rhythm? | NO | YES |
| 19. Would you like to enrich your understanding and enjoyment of orchestral music? | NO | YES |
| 20. Have you more than the normal amount of nervous energy? | NO | YES |

Total of each column:

Score:

# The Drumkit

## Information Sheet

Drummers are born, not made. The drumkit is largely self-selecting; it does not appeal to most people as a way of making music. Whilst almost everyone has a sense of rhythm, that alone is not enough to play the kit.

The kit-player must have *excellent* nervous and muscular co-ordination, which has something to do with why he is a bit of a fidget. He must have a multi-track brain, able to play several rhythmic patterns at the same time using both hands, both feet and sometimes mouth as well. It's a bit like the old party game of revolving one hand clockwise above your head, the other anti-clockwise in front of the chest, whilst tapping left and right feet alternately. Anyone who cannot do that will never learn to play the kit.

Drummers are unusual people. They never quite feel that they belong to the group or band, however much the group needs them—and they need it—in order to make music. No other players sympathize with the drummer's problems, because no one else understands them. Many drummers have a self-protective sense of humour. Those who don't, tend to develop one.

Drummers are meticulous, obsessive. If a violinist, a trombonist and a drummer arrive at a rehearsal together, the first two have only to take an instrument out of its case and they are ready to play. The drummer must spend ten minutes carrying in all his gear and half an hour putting it together before he is ready to play. Each on its special stand, he assembles side drum, bass drum and pedal, two or more tom-toms, crash cymbals, hi-hats and pedals, plus maybe woodblocks, tambourines, triangles, whistles, bangers and clangers. Each instrument has one or more special beater, which must be placed in exactly the right spot to be found while playing—within millimetres. Is that you?

It is normal to begin by learning the side drum with a self-tutor book, but most drummers buy some lessons on side drum technique and the use of the kit as a whole. They practise a lot at home and would go mad without a garage or reasonably sound-proof room to work in. The rest of the family may have to put up with a bit of noise, but regards this as a small price to pay, for playing the kit discharges that strange combination of nervous and physical energy which otherwise exhibits itself in irritability and outbursts of temper.

Acquiring sufficient basic technique to be able to play with others takes about a year. Thereafter, the good amateur drummer is greatly in demand, with a wide range of music he can choose to play, since almost every combination of musicians needs a kit —even the orchestra on occasions.

Social opportunities: Everything except Classical and chamber music.
Method of Learning: Self-tutor books and some private lessons.

# THE DRUMKIT

## *Score Card*

| | SCORE ZERO | SCORE 5 EACH | SCORE 10 EACH |
|---|---|---|---|
| 1. Do you normally sleep (a) LESS THAN 6½ HOURS A NIGHT (b) 6½–7½ (c) MORE THAN 7½? | (c) | (b) | (a) |
| 2. Do any of these names mean something to you: LUDWIG, PREMIER, PAISTE? | NO | YES | |
| 3. When you are tense, do you find yourself drumming fingers or tapping a foot? | NO | | YES |
| 4. As a child, were you hyperactive? | NO | YES | |
| 5. If you hear the first part of a simple rhythmic pattern, do you instinctively complete it? (E.g. boom ditty boom boom—BOOM BOOM!) | NO | YES | |
| 6. Are you basically (a) IMPULSIVE or (b) SOBER, CAUTIOUS? | (b) | (a) | |
| 7. Would you like to play a melodic instrument, i.e. one which plays tunes? | YES | NO | |
| 8. Can you (a) SIT QUIETLY READING A BOOK FOR HOURS or (b) ALWAYS FIND SOME REASON TO BE "ON THE GO"? | (a) | (b) | |
| 9. Have you always fancied playing the drums? | NO | | YES |
| 10. Have you any problems co-ordinating hands, feet, wrists etc? | YES | NO | |
| 11. Can you name three famous drummers? | NO | YES | |
| 12. If you hear the music of a favourite song, do you (a) SING THE PROPER WORDS or (b) SCAT-SING, MAKING UP YOUR OWN SOUNDS? | (a) | (b) | |
| 13. Have you ever enjoyed playing a percussion instrument in cadet band, military or marching band or elsewhere? | NO | | YES |
| 14. Have you ever suffered from arthritis, rheumatism, back/neck/shoulder pains? | YES | NO | |

15. On the kit, a drummer often plays several different rhythms at the same time. Can you tap four-in-a-bar with the right hand against two with the left foot and one with the left hand?

16. Which group of names means more to you? (a) ROSTROPOVICH, BRITTEN, HALLE or (b) KRUPA, HENDRIX, RONNIE SCOTT'S

17. If you played in a group or band, would you prefer to be (a) ONE OF A SECTION ALL PLAYING THE SAME INSTRUMENT or (b) THE ONLY ONE ON YOUR INSTRUMENT?

18. Do you have a much-played collection of records/cassettes featuring the drums?

Total of each column:

Score:

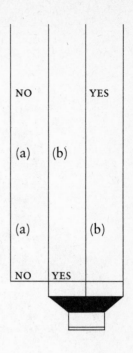

## The BEST-OF-BOTH-WORLDS instruments

"... offer the best of both worlds, for they can be played in orchestras, bands and chamber music ensembles, yet can also be pleasurable and satisfying to play on one's own."

Three different kinds of people achieve comparatively high scores on instruments in this group.

The music-lover who would like to make music alone, yet is not attracted to a ONE-MAN-BAND instrument, will find here an instrument which has a life-time's repertoire of pieces to play alone, from beginner's to concerto standard.

The sociable music-lover who is not attracted to any JOIN-THE-BAND instrument, will find here an orchestral instrument which —after a year or so to acquire basic technique—will become a passport giving entry to amateur orchestras, chamber groups, operatic societies and concert bands.

The quietly sociable also find what they are looking for here: an instrument to play peacefully on their own at home and occasionally in the company of like-minded friends in amateur orchestra or chamber ensemble.

High Scores required in:

| | Flute<br>Clarinet | Oboe<br>Bassoon<br>French Horn | Violin<br>Viola<br>Cello |
|---|---|---|---|
| *RIGHT TIME TEST* | | √ | √ |
| *MUSICALITY TEST* | | √ | √ |
| *SKILL &*<br>*MOTIVATION TEST* | √ | √ | √ |

Note: No High Scores required for the Recorder

# The Woodwind Instruments

## Information Sheet

The woodwind group of orchestral instruments is an odd collection. Unlike the brass, or the strings, which are all variations on one basic idea, the woodwind have little in common except that they were originally all made of wood and are sounded by the player's breath, or wind.

Although often played together in orchestra and chamber group, the two highest instruments—flute and oboe—could not be more dissimilar. The flautist blows whole lungfuls of air across the open hole in the head-joint, so that most of the breath is "wasted". The oboeist, on the other hand, must force tiny quantities of air through a very narrow reed under great pressure. The oboe is held in what looks like a comfortable and logical position in front of the body, while the flute is held horizontally, with the hands out of sight while playing.

The bassoon is really a large oboe designed to produce lower notes, while the clarinet, which was invented later, has a single reed fixed to a chunky mouthpiece and a completely different logic. Even the familiar recorder is a member of the woodwind group, but a comparatively inefficient one which produces too little sound to compete in orchestra or band. The saxophone is the odd man out: a woodwind instrument made of brass.

To play any woodwind instrument requires all the fingers of both hands, sometimes in very complicated "cross-fingerings". Finger co-ordination is far higher than on the brass; lip control is much easier. Thanks to the mechanical aid of all those shiny keys and rods, no high degree of musicality is called for in pitching these instruments and their music is not difficult to read, since they play single notes, never chords.

The reed instruments—oboe, clarinet and bassoon—are played with the reed or mouthpiece inside the mouth. Some people do not take to this idea, those with sensitive teeth or gums actually finding the vibration unpleasant. Playing any woodwind instrument is mildly energetic, on the level of a good yoga session, but the physically frail can find them stressful—particularly the reed instruments.

The well-suited and well-motivated adult swiftly achieves the satisfaction of playing tunes on either flute or clarinet. On the bassoon, this takes longer and the oboe is the most difficult to learn. With or without a local orchestra or chamber group to join, there is a lifetime's repertoire to play at home. All these instruments are easily transportable and none is so loud as to disturb the neighbours.

Some amateur woodwind-players wish only to play tunes, alone; others find their musical satisfaction sitting quietly in orchestral sections contributing their notes to the composite sound. Two very different kinds of playing, yet some players enjoy them both equally and they epitomize having the Best of Both Worlds.

*It is useful to measure the general suitability or otherwise, of the Woodwind for you, before considering each individual instrument.*

*Use the Score Card overleaf to determine your Woodwind Instruments Rating.*

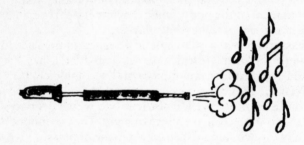

# WOODWIND INSTRUMENTS RATING

|  | SCORE −5 EACH | SCORE ZERO | SCORE +5 EACH |
|---|---|---|---|
| 1. Have you ever enjoyed playing the recorder? | NO | | YES |
| 2. Can you read simple notation? | | NO | YES |
| 3. Do you want an instrument which can play tunes? | | NO | YES |
| 4. Playing a woodwind instrument requires very good finger-control. Would this be a problem for you? | YES | | NO |
| 5. Do you have any trouble with your teeth or gums? | YES | NO | |
| 6. Do you habitually sing or hum to yourself, when alone or concentrating? | | NO | YES |
| 7. Do you have plenty of physical energy? | NO | | YES |
| 8. Do you prefer powerful instruments which make a lot of sound? | YES | NO | |
| 9. Have you suffered from migraines, sinusitis or respiratory problems during the last few years? | YES | NO | |
| 10. Are you a medium or heavy smoker? | YES | NO | |
| Total of each column: | − | ZERO | + |
| Your Woodwind Rating: | | | |

*Notes:*
    1. *To score, see notes on p. 49.*
    2. *You will need this Rating when scoring each of the Woodwind Instruments. If it is positive, add it; if negative subtract it.*

# THE FLUTE

## *Information Sheet*

The flute is perhaps the most natural of all instruments for the average healthy adult body. People have been playing flutes all over the world for many thousands of years because the basic instrument is easy to make and easy to play. Anyone who was baffled by their lack of progress in childhood piano lessons, will be amazed by the swiftness of progress on the flute. No part of the body needs to be taught new tricks in order to play this instrument. Anyone who can purse the lips—as if blowing some dust off the table—and produce a sound when blowing across the hole in a flute head-joint, can learn to make music on the flute.

A healthy mouth is important: the player has only the teeth and lips to control the stream of air—unlike on the other woodwind, where the reed is a mechanical "aid".

The orchestral flute that we know looks much more complicated than the simple un-keyed folk flutes, but the effect of all the rods and keys is to extend the range of the instrument to roughly double that of most people's voices. On the flute, you can soon play melodies which you could sing only in your wildest musical dreams.

Although the sound of the flute is gentle, playing it demands more energy than might be thought, for most of the player's breath passes over the open hole. Anyone with chronic shortness of breath or heart trouble may find this stressful. An adult in normal health gets dizzy after blowing for a few minutes, but gradually builds up lung capacity by practising, in which case the flute is health-promoting. A reasonable amount of regular practice leaves the amateur flautist with a glowing feeling, as though after a good yoga session. Some very left-handed people, and those who need to see what their fingers are doing, are unhappy with the position of the hands when playing: out of sight to the right of the body.

Virtually all orchestral music includes flute parts. The solo repertoire is inexhaustible, including music in many different styles and from all periods. Assembled, the flute measures over two feet in length, but it comes to pieces for carrying and fits into an overcoat pocket or a shoulder bag.

With regular lessons, most adults can within a few months

realize their frustrated dreams of making real music. Without lessons, or with occasional ones, this will take much longer. Also, the self-taught amateur runs the risk of acquiring bad playing habits which can be difficult to break. However, many adults teach themselves the flute satisfactorily, using one or more of the excellent tutor-books.

Social opportunities: Virtually limitless, from Baroque to folk, jazz and pop.

Method of learning: Preferably with regular lessons to begin with, but also self-taught with tutor-books and perhaps occasional lessons.

# THE FLUTE

*Score Card*

| | SCORE ZERO | SCORE 5 EACH | SCORE 10 EACH |
|---|---|---|---|
| 1. Do you enjoy dancing or moving to music? | NO | | YES |
| 2. Are you particularly attracted to the gentle sound of the flute? | NO | | YES |
| 3. The flute presses against the player's lower lip and gum. Are your gums in good condition? | NO | YES | |
| 4. Are your lips *(a)* THIN, (b) AVERAGE or (c) THICK? | (c) | (a) | (b) |
| 5. Have you ever enjoyed singing in a choir? | NO | YES | |
| 6. Do you dislike the idea of putting part of the instrument *inside* your mouth? (e.g. the reed of bassoon or oboe, or the mouthpiece of the clarinet) | NO | | YES |
| 7. Do you lisp or have any speech problem? | YES | NO | |
| 8. Is your voice (a) HIGH, (b) MEDIUM or (c) LOW? | (c) | (b) | (a) |
| 9. Do you want an instrument where you can clearly see your fingers whilst playing? | YES | NO | |
| 10. Which sound do you prefer: (a) PIANO or (b) VIOLIN? | (a) | (b) | |
| 11. Is your left arm long enough to stretch right across the body until the left hand is level with the right ear lobe, *without* twisting your neck? | NO | YES | |

12. If you had to run a
hundred yards or blow up half
a dozen balloons, would you
be (a) VERY OUT OF BREATH (b)
A LITTLE PUFFED or (c)
BREATHING NORMALLY?

(a)    (b)    (c)

Total of each column:

Combined total:
Add/Subtract your Woodwind Rating:
Score:

# THE CLARINET

*Information Sheet*

The idea of playing the oboe or bassoon appeals to very few people. If you wish to take up a woodwind instrument, in most cases it will be either flute or clarinet.

The choice is made easier by the fact that this is an "either/or" situation. If you cannot produce a sound by blowing over the hole in a flute, you will probably be reassured by the feel of the clarinet mouthpiece when firmly gripped between upper teeth and lower lip. On the other hand, if you do not fancy the idea of having part of the instrument inside your mouth, you should be able to make a sound on the flute. In terms of the playing posture for the two instruments, most people instinctively prefer either the "wide open" feeling of holding and blowing a flute or the tight, tidy position of the clarinettist, with the instrument neatly in front of the body and the hands well in view. The flute sounds gentle yet takes a lot of energy to blow; the clarinet requires less energy, yet produces more sound.

If you like the sensation of the reed "buzzing" in the mouth and find the playing position natural and have good finger co-ordination (better than required for the flute), progress on the clarinet can be almost as rapid as on the flute. The logic of fingering the other woodwind instruments, including the sax, is based on the recorder. The clarinet is different, so prior knowledge of the recorder is no help on this instrument.

Quick-witted fast-movers are attracted by the clarinet—perhaps by the possible speed of playing, but also by the penetrating quality of the sound. The clarinet has a greater range of notes than the flute, particularly at the bottom end. Many men prefer the lower-sounding clarinet to the slightly higher flute, as its lower register approximates to their own voices. A mental-arithmetic brain is helpful to read and play clarinet music.

Where the shy and retiring can be happy on the flute, those who like subtly to slip into the limelight from time to time prefer the clarinet. The orchestral clarinettist will need to have had lessons, but many band clarinettists are self-taught. For carrying to orchestra or band practice, the clarinet—like flute and oboe—packs away into a small carrying case. After the initial learning period, many amateur clarinettists practise only once or twice a week—less often than the average amateur flautist.

Social opportunities: Any orchestra or band playing music from Mozart onwards. Chamber music. Jazz.

Method of learning: As on the flute, the best progress is made with regular lessons to begin with, yet many adults manage to teach themselves quite satisfactorily.

## Score Card

| | SCORE ZERO | SCORE 5 EACH | SCORE 10 EACH |
|---|---|---|---|
| 1. The clarinet is versatile, playing many different kinds of music, from Classical to pop. Does this attract you? | NO | | YES |
| 2. Are you impatient, the sort of person who needs quick results? | NO | | YES |
| 3. Would you fancy joining an amateur orchestra, wind band, jazz or dance band? | NO | YES | |
| 4. Do you have your own front teeth, and are they quite strong and healthy? | NO | | YES |
| 5. When playing the clarinet, you feel the reed vibrating inside your mouth. Would you mind this? | YES | | NO |
| 6. Each note has a different fingering on the clarinet. Are you good with your fingers, e.g. at model-making, embroidery? | NO | YES | VERY |
| 7. Do you have a short hand-span or very narrow finger tips? | YES | NO | |
| 8. Would you describe yourself as bright and alert, rather than reflective and dreamy? | NO | | YES |
| 9. Can you remember the name of one famous clarinettist? | NO | YES | |
| 10. Do you want an instrument where you can clearly see your fingers whilst playing? | NO | YES | |
| 11. Which group of composers' names means more to you: (a) QUANTZ, SCARLATTI, TELEMANN or (b) MOZART, WEBER, GERSHWIN? | (a) | (b) | |

12. If you hear a catchy tune, do you "jig around" in time to the music?

| NO | YES |  |
|----|-----|--|

Total of each column:

Combined total:
Add/Subtract your Woodwind Rating:
Score:

# THE OBOE

## Information Sheet

Oboeists are born, not made. Very few of them, amateur or professional, have ever been in two minds as to whether to play the oboe or another instrument. Single-mindedness, or stubbornness are characteristics of oboe-players.

Unquestionably, the oboe does have some of the most beautiful tunes in the Classical repertoire. It can produce the pathos and intensity of the violin. A good amateur oboeist is always in demand for orchestral and chamber music.

In the hands of an outstanding professional player, the oboe sounds sublime, but it is his artistry that makes it so. The essential difficulties of the instrument ensure that the noise made by the amateur learner sounds like a cross between a duck in pain and an angry tomcat. It will take a year or more before tone begins to come, and then only after a lot of hard work. What drives the oboeist on is that he or she is a forward-looking person who appreciates that uphill struggle leads . . . uphill. It is not important to him or her that getting to the level of being able to play with others takes two or three times as long on the oboe as on flute or clarinet.

The amateur oboeist must be prepared to travel to a good teacher, pay for regular weekly lessons and rarely miss one. He or she must also practise for half an hour or more every day. In addition, time will eventually have to be set aside for reed-making, a demanding art in itself.

If none of that is surprising, it may be a shock to learn that the oboe should only be considered by physically fit people. Although, to the casual glance, the position of the oboeist looks like that of the clarinettist, the pressure of playing the oboe is considerable: the player spends the whole time forcing air through the tiny gap between two pieces of stiff reed. The back-pressure is felt in the head, the throat and the lungs, if not throughout the whole body. This instrument is not recommended for anyone who suffers from headaches, sinusitis, neck, chest or back trouble, nor those with high blood pressure.

While there are no easy rewards or quick satisfactions on this instrument, that never seems to worry the oboeists. They work for months and years towards a goal that justifies all the hard work: an endless repertoire of Classical and other orchestral and chamber music.

Social opportunities: Amateur symphony, opera and chamber orchestras. Wind bands. Chamber music.

Method of learning: Only by regular lessons from a professional teacher.

# THE OBOE

## Score Card

|  | SCORE ZERO | SCORE 5 EACH | SCORE 10 EACH |
|---|---|---|---|
| 1. Listening to an orchestra, are you very aware of the oboe's sound? | NO |  | YES |
| 2. Are you looking for a "serious" instrument, difficult to learn and demanding to play? | NO |  | YES |
| 3. Do you suffer from headaches, migraine or sinusitis? | YES | NO |  |
| 4. Do you listen almost exclusively to orchestral and chamber music? | NO |  | YES |
| 5. Would you describe yourself as "highly strung" or neurotic? | NO | YES |  |
| 6. The oboeist grips the narrow reed between the lips, folded back over the teeth. This is difficult for thick lips. Are your lips (a) THICK, (b) AVERAGE or (c) THIN? | (a) | (b) | (c) |
| 7. Would you like to join an amateur orchestra or chamber group? | NO | YES |  |
| 8. Do you have any chest (heart, lung) problems? | YES | NO |  |
| 9. For at least the first year of learning, the oboe sounds discouraging. Are you sufficiently strong-willed to persevere this long before making a pleasant sound? | NO |  | YES |
| 10. Can you manage to practise half an hour minimum each day? | NO | YES |  |
| 11. Have you passed examinations on any other musical instrument? | NO | YES |  |

12. It is not possible to learn the oboe properly without regular lessons. Would you be prepared to pay for oboe lessons?

| NO | YES |
|----|-----|

Total of each column:

Combined total:
Add/Subtract your Woodwind Rating:
Score:

# The Bassoon

*Information Sheet*

Although mechanically, the bassoon is a big oboe, it attracts players very unlike oboeists and far more like tuba-players and bassists, who are bassoonists' counterparts in brass and strings. Most amateur bassoonists have previously learnt piano or sung the lower parts in choirs. The ability to read bass clef may be helpful, but more to the point is their enjoyment of the harmonic role of the lower voices or instruments in a composite sound. They are essentially people who do not want to dominate by singing or playing the top parts.

Physically, this instrument is less stressful than the oboe, because the gap in the reed is—like everything else on the bassoon—larger and therefore easier to blow through. Although the bassoon is as long as many players are tall, it does pack away into a carrying case no larger than a violin-case. An adult of average height or more can be comfortable holding and playing the bassoon, but broad finger-tips and a wide hand-span are necessary in order to reach and cover the keys and holes. Both hands are out of sight while playing.

Bassoons are expensive, compared with the other woodwind: about four times what one would pay for a similar-quality flute.

Those who know the bassoon only in its orchestral role —essentially harmonic with occasional solos—are pleasantly surprised at the extensive and progressive repertoire for the bassoonist to enjoy at home, alone. Although large, the instrument does not sound loud, but rather warm and mellow. The player feels the music through the whole body. It is, after the initial learning period, a warm and generous instrument.

Since there are never sufficient amateur bassoonists, the keen learner who can read music fluently has no problems finding an orchestra or chamber group to join. Progress to this level may take no longer than a year, if regular lessons with a good teacher are available.

| | |
|---|---|
| Social opportunities: | Chamber groups. Amateur symphony, opera and chamber orchestras. Wind bands. Military and concert bands. |
| Method of learning: | Regular, but not necessarily weekly, lessons for the first year or so. |

## Score Card

| | SCORE ZERO | SCORE 5 EACH | SCORE 10 EACH |
|---|---|---|---|
| 1. Are you prepared to spend £600 or more on a reasonable-quality instrument to learn on? | NO | | YES |
| 2. Do you want, and are you able, to have regular lessons from a teacher? | NO | YES | |
| 3. Are you physically quite large? | NO | YES | |
| 4. Have you ever enjoyed singing bass or alto parts in choir, at school, etc? | NO | | YES |
| 5. Are you interested in learning an instrument which plays almost exclusively Classical and chamber music? | NO | | YES |
| 6. Can you read bass clef notation? | NO | YES | |
| 7. Are your hands large, with a wide span and broad finger tips? | NO | | YES |
| 8. Did you learn the piano to examination standard? | NO | YES | |
| 9. The bassoonist rarely plays tunes. Would you be satisfied by an instrument which is only occasionally "in the limelight"? | NO | | YES |
| 10. You cannot see what your fingers are doing, when playing the bassoon. Would this bother you? | YES | NO | |
| 11. Is your voice (a) LOW, (b) MIDDLE or (c) HIGH? | (c) | (b) | (a) |
| 12. Which adjective applies more to you: (a) QUICK-WITTED or (b) CONSCIENTIOUS? | (a) | (b) | |

Total of each column:

Combined total:
Add/Subtract your Woodwind Rating:
Score:

97

# THE RECORDER

## Information Sheet

Only once in the whole System should you fill in a Score card *before* reading the relevant Information Sheet. Do the recorder test now, before reading on.

Most adults are surprised at their score for this instrument. Those with low scores cannot believe it. "If so many children learn to play the recorder, obviously I could"—is their reaction. They are right, but the point of the Score Cards is not to find out whether one could play a particular instrument. The Score Cards are for comparison, to show which instrument will best satisfy an adult's needs, and on which he is most likely to succeed.

Two very different groups of adults tend to score highly enough to have the recorder on their Short Lists.

The first group is made up of those who consciously choose the recorder because they are interested in and attracted to Early Music and the Baroque period. After learning, or brushing up, basic recorder technique on the descant recorder, they can move on to treble and/or tenor recorder, with the aim of playing Handel sonatas with a keyboard, joining a recorder consort or building up an eclectic repertoire of music to play at home (much early woodwind music was originally written for recorder). Evening classes, holiday courses and informal chamber groups give contact with other like-minded music-lovers.

The second group with high scores are, broadly speaking, those who under-estimate their instrumental potential. They love music. They listen to it a great deal. Yet, for whatever reason, they would not feel justified in spending the sort of money involved in buying, say, a flute or clarinet and paying for private lessons. The descant recorder is the one instrument on which you can get started for under £10. That sum will enable you to buy a student-quality wooden instrument (avoid the cheaper plastic ones) and one of the excellent self-tutor books, to use at your own pace of learning in the privacy of the home.

Any adult who enjoys music can teach himself or herself basic recorder technique. How long it takes depends, of course, on the amount of time and energy available and the regularity of practice. The more energy you put in, the more rapid the progress.

Within six months, the average self-taught learner acquires

basic playing technique on a real instrument through his own efforts *and* painlessly absorbs the elements of musical notation. It is a good idea then to work right through the System again, including the Preliminary Tests. The results can be radically different, when it is possible to answer YES to questions like: "Can you read simple notation?" and "Did you ever enjoy learning the recorder?"

Social opportunities: Evening classes. Recorder ensembles. Duets with keyboard. Baroque ensembles. Early Music groups. Holiday courses.

Method of learning: Basic technique usually self-taught or learnt at evening classes. Advanced technique through private lessons, holiday courses, etc.

# THE RECORDER

## Score Card

| | SCORE ZERO | SCORE 5 EACH | SCORE 10 EACH |
|---|---|---|---|
| 1. Is the amount of money you could allocate to buying an instrument limited to less than £10? | NO | YES | |
| 2. Do you enjoy Early Music and Baroque? | NO | | YES |
| 3. Do you find the sound of the recorder (a) PURE, (b) PLEASANT or (c) BORING? | (c) | (b) | (a) |
| 4. Can you name two famous recorder-players? | NO | YES | |
| 5. Do you want an instrument which you can begin to learn alone, without a teacher or the need for paid lessons? | NO | YES | |
| 6. Do you have SOME, MANY or NO recordings of Early Music or other recorder music? | NO | SOME | MANY |
| 7. Did you do well on the recorder at school and/or move on from the descant to another recorder? | NO | | YES |
| 8. Are you (a) A RISK-TAKER or (b) SOMEONE WHO LIKES TO "BACK IT BOTH WAYS"? | (a) | (b) | |
| 9. Which characteristic do you admire: (a) SELF-CONTROL or (b) FLAMBOYANCE? | (b) | | (a) |
| 10. Do you like the sound of electric instruments, e.g. guitar or organ? | YES | NO | |

11. Do you find manual hobbies a relief from mental pressures, e.g. gardening, modelling, woodwork, needlework, etc?

12. Are you a very "careful" person with money?

Total of each column:

Combined total:
Add/Subtract your Woodwind Rating:
Score:

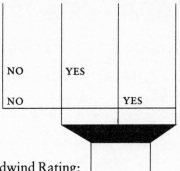

# THE FRENCH HORN

*Information Sheet*

Although made of brass and technically similar in construction to the other brass instruments, the French Horn appeals to a person very different from the easy-going types who choose a brass instrument in order to Join The Band.

The French Horn is an extremely difficult instrument to learn and to play. It never becomes easy—not even for professional players. Without moving a finger on the valves, a very good player can produce on demand any one of twenty different notes, by extremely fine lip-control allied to an exceptionally fine sense of pitch.

This is not a brass band instrument; it plays solo, orchestral and chamber music. In chamber groups, the horn plays with strings, the piano, in brass ensembles and with the woodwind in wind quintets. Musically, it has more in common with the woodwind than any other group of instruments, although the basic feedback of playing is the vibration of lips against mouthpiece—akin to that of the trumpet.

The French Horn has a large range of notes, from very high to very low. There are only three valves to assist the player, so that most of the work is done by his lip and ear. The back-pressure on the player's throat, lungs and diaphragm is considerable, which makes the instrument ill-advised for anyone suffering from headaches, chest or abdominal problems. *Perfect* teeth and gums are required. Most adult beginners who succeed on the horn have previously studied another instrument or had vocal training. A trained sense of pitch and the ability to read music fluently are virtually prerequisites to beginning the French Horn.

The compensation for the great difficulty of this instrument lies in the pleasure of producing its unique and characteristic sound and in the wealth of horn music written by the great composers from Mozart onwards.

New and second-hand instruments are very expensive and there are no quick results on the horn, so it is essentially a long-term investment of time and money for the quiet, intelligent and persistent music-lover who wants—and can devote the time to—such a demanding hobby.

Social opportunities: Symphony, opera and chamber orchestras. Military and wind bands. Wind quintets. Brass ensembles. Mixed chamber music ensembles.

Method of learning: Regular lessons from a professional teacher for the first two or three years; thereafter daily practice and occasional lessons.

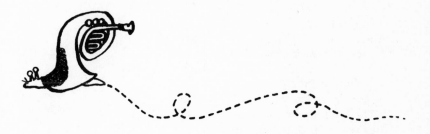

# The French Horn

*Score Card*

| | SCORE ZERO | SCORE 5 EACH | SCORE 10 EACH |
|---|---|---|---|
| 1. Have you previously studied one or more musical instruments? | NO | | YES |
| 2. Are you interested in orchestral and chamber music? | NO | YES | |
| 3. Have you ever enjoyed singing in choirs? | NO | YES | |
| 4. Do you want an easy-to-learn instrument? | YES | NO | |
| 5. Do you find the sound of the French Horn particularly beautiful? | NO | YES | |
| 6. Are you prepared to pay for regular lessons on this instrument from a trained teacher for two or three years? | NO | YES | |
| 7. Have you an excellent sense of pitch? (a) NO or DON'T KNOW (b) YES | (a) | | (b) |
| 8. Do you suffer from headaches or migraine? | YES | NO | |
| 9. Would you want an instrument which will always demand conscientious practice, several times a week? | NO | | YES |
| 10. Are your teeth and gums in perfect condition? | NO | | YES |
| 11. Are you (a) CAREFUL or (b) EASY-GOING, ABOUT YOUR PERSONAL POSSESSIONS? | (b) | (a) | |

| | | |
|---|---|---|
| 12. Are you a quietly determined, introverted person who is looking for a demanding yet fulfilling leisure interest? | NO | YES |
| 13. Do you suffer from any of the following: hernia, piles, heart or respiratory problems, or are you/have you been a heavy smoker? | YES | NO |
| 14. Would you prefer (a) READING A GOOD BOOK QUIETLY AT HOME or (b) BEING IN A CROWDED PUB WITH SOME FRIENDS? | (b) | (a) |
| 15. Do you have any nervous or muscular problems with either hand? | YES | NO |
| 16. Which characteristic would you rate more highly: (a) PERSEVERANCE or (b) GENEROSITY? | (b) | (a) |
| 17. Are your lips (a) THICK, or (b) AVERAGE/THIN? | (a) | (b) |
| 18. Could you definitely make time almost every day, for practice? | NO | YES |
| 19. Do you dislike sudden loud noises? | NO | YES |
| 20. Can you recall the names of two or more French Horn players? | NO | YES |

Total of each column:

Score:

*Note: Do not add or subtract your Woodwind or Brass Rating.*

# THE STRINGED INSTRUMENTS

*Information Sheet*

This group of instruments includes the Second Most Hated Instrument in the World: after the piano, the violin has been associated with more traumatic musical accidents than any other instrument. For totally wrong reasons, hundreds of thousands of children are set to learn this sublime but extremely difficult instrument. They fail, for reasons which have nothing to do with the children or the violin and the memory of failure clings.

If you were traumatized by childhood violin lessons, use the tests in this section simply as reference to compare the other scores. If you never tried to learn a stringed instrument, it is unlikely that you can now succeed on violin or viola, but the cello with its more comfortable and logical playing position may be a possible candidate for your Short List.

Those who did enjoy their childhood violin lessons but have not played for many years, are sometimes discouraged from starting again by vague memories of all the hard work and the slowness of progress. Yet, adults who take courage in both hands and begin again with a proper course of lessons can be very surprised that the work is not so hard as they remembered; it is deeply satisfying to capitalize on all those childhood lessons and practising, as brain and muscles and nerves recall tricks which were thought to be forgotten.

Early violin lessons, if enjoyed and successful, can lead to amateur playing on any stringed instrument. Many adults find that it is simply impossible to get a good position on violin or viola after the joints and sinews begin to stiffen. Most older people lose their perception and pleasure in the higher frequencies, and those with any hearing defect are advised to steer clear of the violin and viola, whose vibrations are carried by bone-conduction into the ear, and can be dangerous. The cello, on the other hand, is an instrument which seems to give more pleasure with increasing years.

It is the cello, too, which attracts adults who did learn a non-stringed instrument but cannot, or do not want to, take up that same instrument. Ex-pianists and wind-players who no longer have sufficient puff re-discover the pleasures of music-making on the cello. Whatever the previous musical experience or education, for an adult to progress on any stringed instrument requires three things: a very good musical ear, the self-discipline to practise regularly and not get discouraged, and regular lessons from a good teacher.

As any music-lover knows, the strings-player needs no rewards other than the endless and inspiring repertoire of music written for his instrument, to be enjoyed at home, in orchestras or chamber groups. Truly, the Best of All Musical Worlds.

*Note:*
*As with the Brass and Woodwind, it is necessary to measure the general suitability of the Strings before considering each individual instrument.*

*Use the Score Card overleaf to determine your Stringed Instruments Rating.*

# STRINGED INSTRUMENTS RATING

| | SCORE −5 EACH | SCORE ZERO | SCORE +5 EACH |
|---|---|---|---|
| 1. Were you one of those children who gave up learning the fiddle after a few terms' unsatisfactory lessons? | YES | NO | |
| 2. Are you a prudent person who is happy to invest time and money now for future enjoyment or security? | NO | | YES |
| 3. Do you generally find orchestral and chamber music unexciting? | YES | NO | |
| 4. Did you enjoy learning a stringed instrument in childhood? | | NO | YES |
| 5. Did you progress to examination level on that instrument? | | NO | YES |
| 6. Have you GOOD, AVERAGE or POOR sense of pitch? | POOR | AVERAGE | GOOD |
| 7. Do you listen seriously to music nearly every day, or do you go regularly to concerts or recitals? | | NO | YES |
| 8. Which characteristic do you rate more higly: (a) FLAIR or (b) CONSCIENTIOUSNESS? | (a) | (b) | |
| 9. Would you be unwilling or unable to have regular weekly lessons for a year or so after taking up a musical instrument? | | YES | NO |
| 10. Do you have any back, shoulder or neck trouble, e.g. fibrositis? | YES | NO | |
| Total of each column: | − | ZERO | + |

Your Strings Rating:

108

*Notes:*
    *1. To score, see notes on p. 49.*
    *2. You will need this Rating when scoring each of the Stringed Instruments. If it is positive, add it; if negative, subtract it.*

# The Violin

*Information Sheet*

The violin is a paradox: it is mechanically the simplest instrument, yet both artistically and intellectually its music is the most difficult to play. A beginner on woodwind or brass can at least produce a few notes which sound good and are satisfying; on the violin, even the most conscientious student may spend two years or more before being able to listen to his own sound with pleasure.

Few people over twenty-five begin the violin from scratch and progress to the level of being able to make real music. Most adults who succeed have previously learnt the violin to examination standard and are still young enough to have the essential suppleness of fingers, wrist and arm which make possible a reasonable playing position. Probably no two people's hearing is the same, but in general as one grows older the perception of higher frequencies becomes less acute. Since every note has to be shaped by the player's sense of pitch, it follows that simply making the notes becomes more difficult as time goes by. The very small dimensions of the instrument are also cruel to adult fingers unaccustomed to precision and speed of reaction. There is simply no fun in "fumbling" on the violin, physically or mentally.

Adults who enjoyed playing the violin when younger, but who gave it up under pressure of examinations, starting a career, family responsibilities, know all the problems in advance. Provided they are prepared to buy regular weekly lessons from a good teacher, to discipline themselves to practise every day without fail, they can, more rapidly than they would have thought, progress past their former level of playing.

Back desk in an amateur orchestra or second violin in an informal string quartet can be possible after a year or so of brushing up one's basic technique. After even a few weeks, as the quality of sound begins to improve, it already becomes pleasurable to build up a home repertoire of old favourites, progressive studies and other bits and pieces of violin music, reflecting the player's preferences and tastes.

As on all instruments, how far the player can progress is directly related to the amount of time available for practice and playing and the amount of mental energy applied. The more time and energy put in, the greater and deeper the rewards.

Social opportunities: Amateur symphony and chamber orchestras. Operatic societies. Mixed chamber music. String quartets. Duets with piano. Some light and folk music. Jazz.

Method of learning: Regular weekly lessons from a professional teacher. Regular daily practice.

# THE VIOLIN

## Score Card

| | SCORE ZERO | SCORE 5 EACH | SCORE 10 EACH |
|---|---|---|---|
| 1. Did you enjoy learning in childhood either (a) VIOLIN or (b) ANOTHER STRINGED INSTRUMENT to approximately Grade IV or V? | NO | (b) | (a) |
| 2. Can you fluently read treble clef notation? | NO | YES | |
| 3. Do you have an excellent sense of pitch? | NO | YES | |
| 4. Do you already have a violin on which you could learn? | NO | | YES |
| 5. Do you enjoy dancing or moving to music? | NO | YES | |
| 6. Have you ever been to a string quartet recital? | NO | | YES |
| 7. Do you have any muscular or nervous trouble with either hand, arm or shoulder? | YES | NO | |
| 8. There are no quick results on the violin. Are you (a) THE SORT OF PERSON WHO EASILY GETS DISCOURAGED or (b) PREPARED TO PLOD ON REGARDLESS? | (a) | | (b) |
| 9. Do you have any hearing defect? | YES | NO | |
| 10. Would you be able and willing to practice every day and miss none, or hardly any, of your regular weekly lessons? | NO | | YES |
| 11. Is your voice (a) LOW or (b) HIGH/MIDDLE? | (a) | (b) | |

12. Since leaving school, have you studied for more than one year to obtain a degree, diploma or professional qualification?

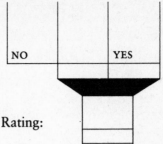

Total of each column:

Combined total:
Add/Subtract your Strings Rating:
Score:

# The Viola

*Information Sheet*

The viola is not a second-class violin. It is a slightly larger and therefore lower-sounding instrument equally important in orchestra or string quartet. Violas rarely play tunes. They spend most of the time harmonizing, or enriching, the tune played on another instrument. Like the middle voices in a choir, viola-players must be content to contribute their harmonies to the composite sound and not seek to dominate it.

The musical role suits a certain kind of person, who is highly musical, very sensitive, responsive—and perhaps above all else a passionate lover of serious music.

Physically, the viola is deceptive. It does not look much larger than the violin but—as anyone knows who has played it—the extra few inches' length of the instrument requires a far longer arm and a healthy neck and back with no aches and pains.

Almost all viola-players began on the violin, so that childhood violin lessons are just as much a preparation for viola as for fiddle. The different stringing, and reading alto clef, do not seem to cause problems for adults. On the contrary, once the player has adjusted to the new clef, the parts are usually easier to read. The larger dimensions of the instrument make it fractionally easier for thickened adult fingers to find the right note.

It can be hard to find a viola teacher, so most students learn from violin teachers. After a few months of regular weekly lessons, it is possible on the viola to ease off and have fortnightly or monthly lessons for the rest of the "brushing-up" period.

There are never enough viola-players in the world to fill the desks in amateur orchestras and chamber groups. Many a Grade V violinist has transferred to the viola and found himself acceptable and welcome in string quartet or orchestra within a few months. If it is possible to say what makes a viola-player, the first thing is to be physically comfortable on the instrument. Secondly, the player must be fulfilled by the harmonic role. Thirdly, there must be a positive attraction to the characteristically melancholy sound of the instrument.

Social opportunities: Amateur symphony and chamber orchestras. Operatic societies. Mixed chamber music. String quartets.

Method of learning: Regular lessons from a professional teacher.

# The Viola

## Score Card

| | SCORE ZERO | SCORE 5 EACH | SCORE 10 EACH |
|---|---|---|---|
| 1. Can you readily name (a) ONE or (b) TWO OR MORE viola-players? | NO | (a) | (b) |
| 2. Would you be frustrated, having an instrument which plays only orchestral and chamber music? | YES | NO | |
| 3. Which composer's music do you prefer: (a) BRAHMS or (b) RAVEL/DON'T KNOW | (b) | (a) | |
| 4. Are your arms short? | YES | NO | |
| 5. Have you previously learnt (a) VIOLIN or VIOLA or (b) ANOTHER STRINGED INSTRUMENT OR PIANO to approximately Grade IV or V? | NO | (b) | (a) |
| 6. Do you have *any* hearing defect? | YES | NO | |
| 7. Have you sung alto, contralto, tenor or baritone in a choir? | NO | | YES |
| 8. Do you ever suffer from fibrositis or any other recurring neck, shoulder or back trouble? | YES | NO | |
| 9. Have you ever been to a string quartet recital? | NO | | YES |
| 10. Are you always cheerful and well-balanced? | YES | NO | |

11. If you were to spend a leisure day with a friend, would you prefer (a) TO MAKE ALL THE DECISIONS or (b) THAT HE OR SHE SHOULD MAKE THEM?

12. Do you have an excellent sense of pitch? (a) YES or (b) NO/DON'T KNOW

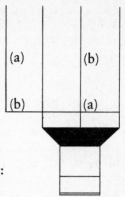

Total of each column:

Combined total:
Add/Subtract your Strings Rating:
Score:

# THE CELLO

*Information Sheet*

Everyone who loves and listens to Classical music has been moved at some time by the sound of the cello. Happily, of all the stringed instruments, this is the one on which an amateur can reasonably aim to make a quality of sound approaching that of professional players. The very first time the bow is pulled across the strings, the cello can make for you a sound which is pleasing, even thrilling, to hear.

The playing position is more natural and comfortable than that for violin or viola. The size of the instrument and the attitude of the left hand make it possible for the adult beginner to acquire a reasonable technique, which is so discouragingly difficult on the fiddle.

There seem to be two avenues by which adults come to the cello. Those who learnt basic strings technique years ago on the violin have to go through an adjustment period for both left hand and bowing, but then find themselves progressing much faster than their memories of the violin would have let them hope. Within a year or so, they are ready for the back desks in amateur orchestras or the less demanding parts in early string quartet music. Those who are able to devote more time to the instrument can push themselves on to a higher level of technique, aiming for the more difficult chamber and solo repertoire.

Some adults, with no previous musical education or experience, also succeed on the cello because they are prepared to work very hard for a long time in order to achieve the pleasure and satisfactions of playing this instrument. Those who had piano or other instrumental instruction, however long ago, or who have sung in choirs seriously, have a great advantage inasmuch as they can concentrate their energy on the technique of the instrument itself, whereas the beginner from scratch must at the same time absorb the rudiments of music.

The only adults who are uncomfortable on the cello are those with small hands, who find the left-hand stretches painful, and some people with back trouble who find it impossible to sit forward on a hard chair for very long, gripping a suitcase-sized object between the knees.

As one grows older, the cello is a good friend. The satisfaction of playing many of the higher-sounding instruments diminishes, while the sound of the cello continues to be just as enjoyable, and its repertoire is inexhaustible. It is truly one of the few instruments as pleasurable to play at seventeen or seventy.

Social opportunities: Amateur symphony and chamber orchestras. Operatic societies. Mixed chamber music. String quartets.

Method of learning: Regular lessons from a professional teacher and conscientious practice.

## Score Card

| | SCORE ZERO | SCORE 5 EACH | SCORE 10 EACH |
|---|---|---|---|
| 1. Can your left hand span an OCTAVE on the piano, or MORE or LESS? | LESS | OCTAVE | MORE |
| 2. Do you get uncomfortable sitting down, perhaps because you have to sit a lot in everyday life? | YES | NO | |
| 3. Can you read bass clef notation? | NO | | YES |
| 4. Have you previously learnt (a) CELLO or (b) ANOTHER STRINGED INSTRUMENT or PIANO, to approximately Grade IV or V? | NO | (b) | (a) |
| 5. When listening to an orchestra or band, are you aware of what the lower instruments are doing? | NO | | YES |
| 6. Do you already own a cello, or are you prepared to spend £250 or more on an instrument to start on? | NO | | YES |
| 7. Can you readily name three or more cellists? | NO | THREE | MORE |
| 8. Is your voice HIGH, MIDDLE or LOW? | HIGH | MIDDLE/LOW | |
| 9. Take a suitcase or other rigid object measuring 15 inches across. This is about the same as the cello. Sit forward on a hard chair and grip the suitcase between your knees. Does this feel uncomfortable? | YES | NO | |

10. Would you be frustrated, having an instrument that plays only orchestral and chamber music?   YES   NO

11. Do you ever suffer from back pain?   YES   NO

12. Do you prefer (a) WORKING UNDER PRESSURE or (b) TAKING YOUR TIME TO GET THINGS RIGHT?   (a)   (b)

Total of each column:

Combined total:
Add/Subtract your Strings Rating:
Score:

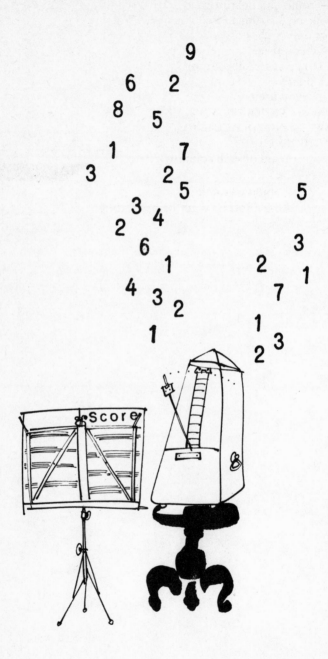

## Comparing Your Scores

After filling in the Score Cards, you may be wondering what exactly the scores signify. Are they high or low? Good or bad? Do they mean a pass or a fail?

The scoring system is purely and simply a numerical way of expressing the comparative suitability of the various instruments for you. It enables you to see at a glance, by entering your scores on the Comparison Chart below, which instruments are most suitable for you to learn and play.

The higher the score, the more suitable the instrument. It does not matter whether your highest scores are in the 60–90 bracket or between 100 and 120. It is the *comparison* of your scores which tells you what you want to know.

The more scores you have, the better the Chart performs its function. Scores for at least two-thirds of the instruments are the minimum necessary for a truly reliable basis of comparison. Should you have less than fifteen scores, fill in a few more Score Cards to give the required minimum.

# SCORING COMPARISON CHART

| INSTRUMENT | SCORE | High scores required in Preliminary Tests: | | |
|---|---|---|---|---|
| | | Right Time Test | Musicality Test | Skill & Motivation Test |
| PIANO .................................. | | ✓ | | ✓ |
| CLASSICAL GUITAR ............... | | ✓ | ✓ | ✓ |
| HARPSICHORD ...................... | | ✓ | ✓ | ✓ |
| ELECTRONIC ORGAN ............. | | | | |
| TRUMPET .............................. | | | ✓ | |
| CORNET ................................ | | | ✓ | |
| TROMBONE ........................... | | | ✓ | |
| TENOR HORN, ETC ................ | | | ✓ | |
| TUBA ................................... | | | ✓ | |
| SAXOPHONE .......................... | | | | ✓ |
| ORCHESTRAL PERCUSSION .... | | | ✓ | |
| DRUMKIT .............................. | | | | ✓ |
| ORCHESTRAL DOUBLE BASS | | | ✓ | ✓ |
| FLUTE .................................. | | | | ✓ |
| CLARINET ............................. | | | | ✓ |
| OBOE ................................... | | ✓ | ✓ | ✓ |
| BASSOON .............................. | | ✓ | ✓ | ✓ |
| RECORDER ............................ | | | | |
| FRENCH HORN ..................... | | ✓ | ✓ | ✓ |
| VIOLIN ................................. | | ✓ | ✓ | ✓ |
| VIOLA .................................. | | ✓ | ✓ | ✓ |
| CELLO .................................. | | ✓ | ✓ | ✓ |

*Notes:*

1. *The completed Comparison Chart reveals clearly the instruments most suitable for you—those for which you have the highest scores and any requisite high scores in the Preliminary Tests.*

2. *Seeing their own results on the Chart surprises some people. They may have a very high score on an instrument they would never have dreamed of playing. Nevertheless, if the Four-Way Matching Process reveals such an instrument as being suitable for them, it is.*

3. *Others are incredulous of a low score on an instrument they have always wanted to play. The low score is due either to having learned facts about the instrument of which they were previously unaware, or because the Four-Way Matching Process has uncovered an incompatibility between them and this particular instrument. It is exactly this kind of hidden pitfall that accounts for the failure of so many adults who take up instruments for vaguely emotional reasons along the lines of "but I've always fancied playing the . . .", rather than as a result of a logical and methodical approach such as this System.*

4. *It can be frustrating to see a number of high-scoring instruments disqualified by lack of requisite high scores in the Preliminary Tests. If the missing high score is for the Right Time Test, it is very possible that a more interesting choice of instruments will be obtained by doing this Test again after a few months, when circumstances may have altered, affecting the score in this Test.*

5. *There is a margin of error in any system. So, if you feel strongly that any of your scores is much too high or too low, compared with the rest, go back and re-read the relevant Information Sheet, then re-do that Score Card. Possibly, knowing what you know about all the instruments may affect your score.*

When you are happily able to accept your scores on the Comparison Chart, there are two possibilities: one is that the highest-scoring instrument immediately "clicks"—you know in your bones that it is the one instrument for you. Perhaps the score is so much the highest that it "sticks out a mile"; perhaps it is an instrument you have always wanted to play, yet previously lacked the courage to attempt; it could be an instrument you enjoyed learning when young, but had not thought of taking up again until the System confirmed its suitability.

125

In such a case, all you have to do is shout "Eureka!", plunder what you need from the Adult Beginner's Information Pack at the back of this book and begin to . . . MAKE MUSIC!

And, supposing you have no such clear-cut result, what then? You continue being logical and systematic: you use the Short List.


*Optional Short List Procedure*

If choosing between a number of possible alternatives is difficult, it is customary to resort to the tried and tested device of the short list. This works equally well when looking for the best candidate for a job, selecting the World Cup football team from the national squad or . . . finalizing the choice of instrument.

By putting the same questions, or applying the same criteria, to each of the possibilities, the short list automatically produces the best overall choice.

Enter below the three instruments which came top of your Chart and for which you have any necessary high scores in the Preliminary Tests. Now, re-read the relevant Information Sheets. After doing that, respond to each question by allotting ten points to the instrument you consider most suitable for yourself, five points to the second choice and zero to the least suitable. Make a clear choice in each case—no equal marks!

| | Short-listed instruments: | | |
| --- | --- | --- | --- |
| | A...... | B...... | C...... |
| 1. Which of these instruments do you find most interesting? | | | |
| 2. Which instrument best suits your mentality as regards learning? (i.e. not too easy, not too difficult) | | | |
| 3. Which instrument plays the kind, or kinds of music you wish to make? | | | |
| 4. The trombone uses no fingers, the piano all ten. Which of these instruments requires the level of digital dexterity you have? | | | |
| 5. Of which of these instruments would you most like to have a collection of recordings? | | | |
| 6. The music written for some instruments is more difficult to play than that for others. Which best suits you? | | | |
| 7. Which of these instruments would best enable you to play in situations where you are happy? (e.g. at home alone or in bands, orchestras, etc) | | | |
| 8. Check the Method of Learning. Which instrument would most easily integrate into your normal life-style, as far as learning it goes? | | | |
| 9. Some instruments require more physical energy than others. Which best matches your spare physical energy? | | | |

| | A...... | B...... | C...... |
|---|---|---|---|
| 10. Which of these instruments would you like to know more about? | | | |
| 11. If you can imagine what kind of person you will be in five years' time, decide which instruments will best suit you then. | | | |
| 12. Some instruments require a lot of time to learn and play; others do not. Which of the three would best fit into your available leisure time? | | | |
| 13. If, when young, you had been offered lessons on these three instruments, which would you have picked? | | | |
| 14. Friends and colleagues will take an interest in your music-making. Which instrument would you prefer to tell them you can play? (Note: To answer the next three questions, you may need to refer to sections in the Adult Beginner's Information Pack) | | | |
| 15. Which instrument is priced in the bracket which you consider a proper amount to pay? (see p. 135) | | | |
| 16. When hearing the instruments played solo by professional musicians, which sound do you most enjoy? | | | |
| 17. Which instrument is most suited to the availability of teachers and/or playing opportunities in your area? (see pp. 136–138) | | | |

| | A...... | B...... | C...... |
|---|---|---|---|
| (Note: Before answering the three final questions, it is necessary to try the instruments for yourself in a music shop. Don't be shy! If you are, choose a large shop and ask to try the portable ones in a private room or cubicle.) | | | |
| 18. After trying all three instruments, which is the most comfortable to hold and play? | | | |
| 19. Do you like the sound you hear when producing a note or two on these instruments? | | | |
| 20. When holding and playing the instruments, which gives you the most pleasant "feedback" or sensation? | | | |
| Totals: | | | |
| Highest-Scoring Instrument: | | | |

And that's it! The highest-scoring instrument is the one on which you can succeed in making music.

You have benefited from an information base that took ten years to research and survey, but, by filling in the Score Cards you have effectively made several thousand discriminatory decisions as between one instrument and another, so all the decisions are your own. It is those decisions which have led you, step by step, to the one instrument which is right for you.

It could be one of the most important discoveries of your life. In a world of increasing leisure, it can make you one of the truly rich, one of the fortunate who need never be bored, depressed, unsatisfied, lonely or frustrated, because YOU CAN MAKE MUSIC.

A mini-directory of information, sources and contact addresses:
  (i) buying and owning an instrument
 (ii) guide to instrument prices
(iii) finding a teacher/paid tuition
(iv) guide to self-tuition publications
 (v) helpful books and magazines
(vi) useful addresses

## (i) buying and owning an instrument

Buying a new instrument

In general, the larger the shop, the greater the range to choose from. Very expensive instruments and the cheaper imported ones are not advised; the latter tend to have irreparable manufacturing faults. See Guide to Instrument Prices for the brackets within which reasonable-quality student models are available.

Buying second hand:
(a) from a music shop

Most larger shops have a range of guaranteed, overhauled used instruments, which may not be on display. The guarantee is part of what you pay for, so prices may not be very much lower than for new instruments. The main advantage of this method of purchase is that it should be possible to get a slightly better-quality instrument for the same outlay.

(b) privately

Private advertisements in shop windows and local newspapers can lead to bargains but also to disastrous purchases of e.g. wrong-pitched instruments and instruments which cannot properly be tuned. Generally, the rule in buying privately is to remember that the greater the number of moving parts in an instrument, the greater the possibility of something being wrong, or going wrong shortly after purchase. For a fee—which can be money well invested—most music shops will check an instrument before purchase.

132

| | |
|---|---|
| Hiring | Many music shops hire out instruments, usually for periods of three months at a time. |
| Hire purchase | A perfectly normal way of buying instruments, especially the higher-priced ones. |
| Hire-and-buy | The most popular way of buying new instruments: the shop hires out the instrument for three months, with an option to buy at the end of this time. If the customer decides to buy, the hire charge is deducted from the purchase price. |
| "Shopping around" | Always a good idea. Prices for the same instrument (or very similar models) can vary from shop to shop. |
| Cash discount | Worth asking for. |
| Borrowing instruments | Brass band instruments are normally borrowed from the band (in forty years' playing, many bandsmen never buy an instrument). |
| | Orchestral percussionists use the orchestra's instruments at rehearsals and performances—some bassists also. |
| Trading-in | Reasonable-quality instruments are always accepted in part-payment for a better instrument, after the initial learning period. Reasonable-quality instruments hold their value better than most other possessions. |
| Electric instruments | Are the one exception to the above rule, for all have built-in obsolescence, particularly keyboards. |

| | |
|---|---|
| Guarantee/warranty | Every new instrument should have a twelve-month manufacturer's guarantee. |
| | When buying second-hand from a shop, ensure that the shop gives an explicit warranty covering parts and labour for a specific period. |
| Repairs | Most larger shops do routine adjustments and non-specialist repairs on the premises. Strings and brass have little to go wrong; the woodwind need repairs more frequently. |
| Insurance of instruments | Effected either through a music shop or a normal insurance agent. |

## *(ii) guide to instrument prices*

1986 U.K. price ranges of reasonable-quality student instruments, suitable for adult learners

| | |
|---|---|
| PIANO | £800–£1000 |
| CLASSICAL GUITAR | £50–£80 |
| HARPSICHORD as kit | £1200 |
| assembled | £1800 |
| ELECTRONIC ORGAN | £150 upwards |
| TRUMPET | £110–£150 |
| CORNET | £130–£160 |
| TROMBONE | £150 upwards |
| TENOR HORN | £230 |
| BARITONE | £330 |
| EUPHONIUM | £380 |
| TUBA | £1300 |
| ALTO SAXOPHONE | £325 upwards |
| TENOR SAXOPHONE | £375 upwards |
| DRUMKIT | £400 upwards |
| ORCHESTRAL DOUBLE BASS | £350 |
| FLUTE | £130–£180 |
| CLARINET | £180–£220 |
| OBOE | £400 upwards |
| BASSOON | £700 upwards |
| RECORDER | £5–£15 |
| FRENCH HORN | £175–£350 |
| VIOLIN | £40–£120 |
| VIOLA | £90–£150 |
| CELLO | £250 upwards |

## (iii) finding a teacher / paid tuition

| | |
|---|---|
| Public Library | Most libraries have a list of instrumental teachers in area. |
| Music shops | Staff know the local teachers. Many shops have teaching studios on the premises, where lessons are given. |
| Local newspapers | Some teachers advertise. Adults who seek tuition also place advertisements. |
| Yellow pages | Include names of teachers and music schools. |
| Schools of Music, Guitar Studios, Organ Centres, etc. | Most towns have one. Students of all ages are normally accepted. Daytime, evening and weekend lessons. When a particular music school offers no tuition on certain instruments, it can usually recommend someone, if asked to do so. |
| Music Centres | Run by school system, mostly on school premises for tuition, orchestral rehearsals of children learning through schools. Main use to adult learners is as source of contacts —staff may also teach private pupils, or know colleagues who do. |
| Evening Institutes, etc. | Evening and daytime group lessons for beginners on some instruments. |
| Incorporated Society of Musicians (I.S.M.) | Publishes Professional Register of Private Teachers of Music. Has sixty local representatives. See Useful Addresses section. |
| Universities, Music Colleges, Training Colleges, Colleges of Further Education, etc. | At any University or college which includes music in its syllabus, staff and advanced students give private lessons. |

| | |
|---|---|
| Professional performing musicians | Many performing musicians teach. Those who do not should be able to recommend colleagues who do. For list of performing musicians in any area, contact firstly the Head Office of the Musicians' Union. All performing musicians must belong to this organization. See Useful Addresses section. |
| Professional orchestras, operatic companies | The orchestra's or company's administrative office will advise which players give tuition, and pass on enquiries. |
| Amateur orchestras and operatic societies | Often include professional players, who teach. Some amateur players also teach, or can give advice about local teachers. |
| Children learning/any local music teacher | Worthwhile asking parents of children learning privately for names of local teachers. A teacher of any instrument can normally introduce colleagues on other instruments. |
| Specialist magazines | Carry teachers' advertisements. See Helpful Books & Magazines section. |
| Church organists/choir-masters/amateur conductors/piano tuners, etc. | Often have a wide range of musical contacts, including teachers. |
| Diplomas, letters after names | The five most popular teaching diplomas are ALCM, ARCM, LRAM, ATCL and AGSM. Many teachers do not have any recognized diploma, yet are as good as or better than those who do. In every case, the teacher's local reputation is as important as any qualification. |

| | |
|---|---|
| Tuition fees | Each private teacher decides his own scale of fees and the length of lesson given. There is no fixed scale of fees and no guarantee that more expensive teachers are better than colleagues who charge less. |
| | The I.S.M. recommends a minimum rate for individual private tuition from a qualified teacher, which for 1986 is £8.60 per hour. Well-known performing musicians tend to charge above this rate; local teachers tend to charge below it. |
| Method of payment | Some teachers require payment for a course of lessons in advance; others prefer to be paid in cash at each lesson. |
| Frequency of lessons | Not necessarily weekly. See Information Sheet for each instrument. |
| Group lessons | The idea of paying less for a group lesson is attractive to some people, but the method is not as successful as individual lessons. Possibly a good idea for beginners on electronic organ and recorder. |
| Amateur and semi-professional players | In brass bands, dance bands, jazz bands, etc, it is customary for experienced amateur and semi-pro players to give some starter lessons, brush-up lessons and tuition on specific points of technique, on an irregular basis for payment. |

138

## (iv) guide to self-tuition publications

There is a wide selection of self-tuition books and systems for most instruments. Not all instruments are recommended for learning without a teacher. Of those which are, the publications below are easy-to-follow, reasonably-priced, do not require previous musical knowledge and are stocked, or obtainable to order, by most music shops. Local shops also recommend publications which are particularly popular with their customers.

ELECTRONIC ORGAN
*The Complete Organ Book:* K. Baker (Wise Publications)
*The Yamaha Organ Book* (Yamaha)

TRUMPET/CORNET
*A Tune A Day for Trumpet or Cornet* (Chappell/Boston)
*Learn As You Play Trumpet* (Boosey & Hawkes)
*Brass For Beginners* (Boosey & Hawkes)
*\*Let's Play Trumpet:* Learning Unlimited (Hal Leonard Publications)

TENOR HORN/BARITONE/EUPHONIUM
*A Tune A Day For . . .* (Chappell/Boston)
*Brass For Beginners* (Boosey & Hawkes)

TUBA/E FLAT, B FLAT BASS
*A Tune A Day For Tuba* (Chappell/Boston)
*\*Let's Play Tuba:* Learning Unlimited (Hal Leonard Publications)
*Brass For Beginners* (Boosey & Hawkes)

SAXOPHONES
*A Tune A Day For Saxophone* (Chappell/Boston)
*A Practical Tutor For The Saxophone:* Otto Langey (Boosey & Hawkes)
*Fun With The Saxophone* (Mel Bay Publications)

139

*Let's Play Alto Saxophone/Let's Play Tenor Saxophone:* Learning Unlimited (Hal Leonard Publications)

ORCHESTRAL PERCUSSION

*A Tune A Day For Marimba, Xylophone & Bells* (Chappell/Boston)

DRUMKIT

*A Tune A Day For The Drums* (Chappell/Boston)
*The First Step Drumkit* (Keith Prowse/EMI)
*Begin To Play Rock & Jazz On The Drum Set:* Feldstein (Alfred Music)
*Let's Play Percussion:* Learning Unlimited (Hal Leonard Publications)

FLUTE

*A Tune A Day For Flute* (Chappell/Boston)
*How To Play The Flute* (Elm Tree Books/EMI)
*Learn As You Play Flute* (Boosey & Hawkes)
*Let's Play Flute:* Learning Unlimited (Hal Leonard Publications)

CLARINET

*A Tune A Day For Clarinet* (Chappell/Boston)
*The Kell Method For Clarinet* (Boosey & Hawkes)
*Learn As You Play Clarinet* (Boosey & Hawkes)
*A Practical Tutor For The Clarinet:* Otto Langey (Boosey & Hawkes)
*Let's Play Clarinet:* Learning Unlimited (Hal Leonard Publications)

140

RECORDER

*Teach Yourself Recorder* (OUP)
*First Step Recorder Book* (Belwyn Mills)
*A Systematic Method For Recorder:* Fred Dinn (Schott)

*Includes pre-recorded cassette of backing material to "play along with".

## (v) useful addresses

| | |
|---|---|
| Amateur Music Association | 43 Renshaw Street, Liverpool |
| Association of Adult Education | Hamilton House, Mabledon Place, London WC1 |
| British Association for Jazz Education | Seymour Mews House, London W1H 9PE |
| British Association of Symphonic Wind Bands & Wind Ensembles | Silver Birches, Bentick Road, Altrincham, Cheshire WA14 2BP |
| British Federation of Brass Bands | 21 Wouds Court, Moira, Burton-on-Trent, Staffs |
| British Flute Society | 7 Cherry Street, Old Town, Stratford-on-Avon CV37 6DF |
| British Jazz Society | 10 Southfield Gardens, Twickenham, Middlesex TW1 4SZ |
| Clarinet & Saxophone Society of Great Britain | 21 Crawford Road, North Wolverhampton |
| Dept. of Education & Science | Elizabeth House, York Road, London SE1 7PH |

| | |
|---|---|
| Dolmetsch Foundation | High Pines, Wood Road, Hindhead, Surrey GU26 6PT |
| European Piano Teachers' Association | 28 Emperor's Gate, London SW7 4HS |
| European String Teachers' Association | 5 Neville Avenue, New Malden, Surrey KT3 4SN |
| Incorporated Society of Musicians | 10 Stratford Place, London W1N 9AE |
| Music Teachers' Association | 198 Park Lane, Macclesfield, Cheshire SK11 6UD |
| Musicians' Union | Head Office: 60–62 Clapham Road, London SW9 0JJ |
| National Association of Percussion Teachers | 1 Gravel Hill Cotts, Swanmore, Hants SO3 2PQ |
| National Federation of Music Societies | Francis House, Francis Street, London SW1P 1DE |
| National Operatic & Dramatic Association | 1 Crestfield Street, London WC1H 8AU |
| Workers' Educational Association | 9 Upper Berkeley Street, London W1H 8BY |

Information about local music-making is also obtainable from the Public Library, the local authority Leisure Services Dept., Art Centres, Regional and sub-Regional Arts Associations, Adult Education Institutes—and from music shops and Schools of Music.

## (vi) books and magazines of interest

### books

> *British Music Education Yearbook* (Rhinegold Publishing)
> *British Music Yearbook* (Rhinegold Publishing)
> *How to Appreciate Music:* Sidney Harrison (Elm Tree
> Books/EMI)
> *How to Read Music:* Roger Evans (Elm Tree Books/EMI)
> *Rudiments and Theory of Music* (Associated Board of the
> Royal Schools of Music)
> *Questions and Exercises on Theory of Music* (Associated
> Board)
> *The Observer's Book of Music:* Freda Dinn (Warne)
> *Everyman's Dictionary of Music:* Eric Blom (Dent)
> *The Musical Companion:* Bacharach & Pearce (Gollancz)

### periodicals

The following periodicals carry various items of interest to the beginner, including teachers' advertisements, notices of performances, reviews of instruments and recordings, particulars of holiday courses, etc.

> *Brass Band News*
> *Crescendo International*
> *Classical Music*
> *Drums & Percussion*
> *Early Music*
> *Guitar*
> *English Harpsichord Magazine*
>
> *Musical Times*
> *Music & Musicians*
> *Music Teacher*
> *Jazz Times*
> *Sounding Brass*
> *The Strad*
> *Recorder & Music*